Paris and Her Remarkable Women

Paris and He

LORRAINE LISCIO

Remarkable Women

THE LITTLE BOOKROOM

NEW YORK

© 2009 The Little Bookroom
Book design: Katy Homans

PUBLISHED BY
The Little Bookroom
435 Hudson Street, 3rd Floor
New York, NY 10014
editorial@littlebookroom.com
www.littlebookroom.com

Library of Congress Cataloging-in-Publication Data

Liscio, Lorraine.
  Paris and her remarkable women / by Lorraine Liscio.
     p. cm.
  ISBN 978-1-892145-77-2 (alk. paper)
  1. Women—France—Paris—Biography. 2. Paris
(France)—History. I. Title.
  HQ1615.A3L57 2009
  920.720944'361—dc22
  [B]
                              2009011570

Front cover: Achille Deveria: Rachel; Comédie Française, Paris,
France / Giraudon / The Bridgeman Art Library International

Frontispiece: Coco Chanel, c. 1930; Bildarchiv Preussischer
Kulturbesitz / Art Resource, NY

Table of Contents

6   Note to the Reader

8   Introduction

11   Geneviève, Patron Saint of Paris (423–502/512?)

19   Héloïse (d. 1164)

27   Christine de Pizan (1364–1431?)

35   Marie de Rabutin-Chantal, Marquise de Sévigné (1626–1696)

41   Françoise d'Aubigné, Madame de Maintenon (1635–1719)

47   Gabrielle Emilie Le Tonnelier de Breteuil, Madame du Châtelet (1706–1749)

55   Marie-Jeanne (Manon) Phlipon, Madame Roland (1754–1793)

63   Elisabeth Vigée Le Brun (1755–1842)

69   Eliza Rachel Félix (1821–1858)

75   Amantine Aurore Lucile Dupin Dudevant / George Sand (1804–1876)

83   Sarah Bernhardt (1844–1923)

91   Camille Claudel (1864–1943)

97   Maria Sklodowska / Marie Curie (1867–1934)

105   Sidonie-Gabrielle Colette (1873–1954)

113   Gabrielle "Coco" Chanel (1883–1971)

119   Simone de Beauvoir (1908–1986)

124   Endnotes

Disappeared?

A number of years ago when I began rooting about in the letters of the twelfth-century Paris scholar and abbess Héloïse, famous consort of philosopher Abélard, I wrote the curator of the Cluny Museum in Paris to ask where the vestiges of her convent were to be found. I had read that some fragments of the original structure were in the museum's permanent collection, but could not find anything during my visit. When I asked the staff, no one seemed to know specifics. (The curator's *documentaliste*'s response, a one-sentence letter, informed me that a double arcade had *indeed* been on display in the Cluny gardens at one time, but was subsequently moved to the Argenteuil Museum in the suburbs where "it has disappeared. Yours truly. . . .")

One summer day, poking around the Cluny as I frequently do, I noticed an arched fragment hung high on a wall, an age-worn bas-relief whose partially beheaded figures were barely decipherable: an angel, Christ(?), and Mary(?). The title below it equivocates: "From Héloïse's convent?"

This anecdote serves as a metaphor for the difficulties involved in tracking down some of history's remarkable women. Often the traces of women said to have disappeared have not; one must only look harder and piece together the clues like a detective. For instance, Christine de Pizan (1364–1431?), well-known to art historians for her illuminated manuscripts but ignored as the first French professional woman author (commissioned biographer of King Charles V, she also wrote poetry, books on good government, arms and chivalry, "the woman question," and more), has been restored to her place in the literary canon by feminist scholars. In an example as recent as 1969, Jacques Cassar, setting out to write his doctoral thesis on poet Paul Claudel, stumbled upon the forgotten name of Paul's sister, Camille Claudel, a sculptor hailed as "one of the glories of France" during her lifetime (she died in 1943); he could not resist making her story public once again. It had not taken long for her to disappear from the popular mind after her death, despite the fact that Rodin designated a room in his museum for her work alone.

And then there are women whose accomplishments have been excised from their stories in order to cast them in stereotypical roles. A case in point is Emilie du Châtelet, commonly known to the French as Voltaire's mistress. In 2006 for the tri-centennial of her birth, the Bibliothèque Nationale in Paris mounted an exhibit on this *"Femme des lumières"* (woman of the Enlightenment), highlighting her translation of and illustrations for works by Newton, Leibniz, and others, as well as a demonstration of her own experiments in physics (including video segments from an American PBS *Nova* program the previous year, "Einstein's Big Idea"), a revelation to many. Now there is an Institut Emilie du Châtelet in the Chaillot Museum of Natural History established for conferences and research on women, sex, and gender. But it is hard to find, no sign anywhere in the building, and the receptionist whom I queried had never heard of it.

Do not give up on women whose traces have "disappeared."

Lorraine Liscio

Out of the Shadows

To visit Paris is to wander through its stories and glimpse its ghosts. The sixteen remarkable women here were protagonists in the stories that shape our understanding of medieval Paris, the sixteenth-century wars of religion, the culture of the Enlightenment, Louis XIV's court, the chaos of the Revolution, the nineteenth-century art scene and theater, and twentieth-century breakthroughs in science, fashion, and feminism.

Each chapter follows one woman to places in Paris pertinent to her life. We accompany revolutionary Manon Roland in the tumbril ride to her execution in Place de la Révolution (now Place de la Concorde); see the grandeur, folly, and macabre side of Louis XIV's court through the eyes of chronicler Madame de Sévigné; peer down the alley where the poorly-funded Marie Curie worked for four years in a dilapidated lab in the Latin Quarter to extract a decigram of radium; watch as Simone de Beauvoir is first praised, then vilified by crowds for her feminist inquiry, *The Second Sex,* at the Left Bank café Les Deux Magots; and traipse with arm-swinging ease through the muck and ooze of Paris streets with novelist George Sand in her *redingote* (riding coat), boots, and top hat when she lived in her house across from Notre Dame.

Other notable sites serve as narrative markers: the vestiges of the medieval tower of the Louvre (in the museum's Sully Wing) where Christine de Pizan, the first French professional woman writer and bookmaker, did her research in Charles V's library; Emilie du Châtelet's spectacular Hôtel Lambert on the Ile Saint-Louis; or the Hôtel d'Albret in the Marais, where a discreet meeting cleared an unlikely path for the indigent widow Françoise Scarron to Louis XIV's marital bed.

The stories of these women aim to open Paris to your imagination. Once aware of the obstacles they overcame, how much more compelling will you find Elisabeth Vigée Le Brun's controversial painting in the Louvre, or Camille Claudel's virtuosic range of sculptures in the Rodin Museum?

When visiting Notre Dame, will you give a nod to the spectral Abélard and Héloïse whose tragic fate was sealed in its shadow? Or scrutinize the enigmatic sculpture of Paris's patron saint Geneviève on the cathedral's façade? As both the legendary "savior" of Paris from the menacing Attila the Hun and the negotiator with the conquering Franks, she has left traces throughout Paris in the most unexpected places.

Elsewhere many readers may have unknowingly already met two of Paris's most electrifying women, both actresses in the Comédie-Française. The first, Rachel, served as the model for Henry James's raw acting talent, Miriam Rooth, in *The Tragic Muse* and for Charlotte Brontë's Vashti, whose fiery performance literally sets the theater ablaze in *Villette*. When the second, Sarah Bernhardt, climbed the proscenium, Parisian critics claimed she was no Rachel. Marcel Proust did not agree and immortalized her as Berma in his novel, *In Search of Lost Time.* (The Théâtre de la Ville at Châtelet is the Théâtre Sarah Bernhardt.)

Even those women whom you thought you knew may prove surprising. Would you have ever thought of Marie Curie as a home-breaker and threat to the nation, as many French accused? Or guess from Coco Chanel's boutique today on rue Cambon that her designs (now by Karl Lagerfeld) simplified and increased the comfort of women's fashion? Fed up with sartorial encumbrances, she quipped that coutouriers had forgotten there were women inside their dresses. And what are we to make of Emilie du Châtelet, whom the French know as Voltaire's mistress and not as a groundbreaking scientist?

For all the talented women here the common conundrum of their lives was how to navigate the tides of custom, law, and resources; and for all, Paris made that possible. Since most guidebooks speak predominantly of men, I turn the spotlight on Paris and her women. By summoning these extraordinary women from the shadows throughout the city (shadows of time and shadows of neglect as women), I let them stand out alone or beside their celebrated male counterparts. After all, when visiting Paris, the more ghosts one meets, the better.

Geneviève

(423–502/512?)

PATRON SAINT OF PARIS, GALLO-
ROMAN NOBLEWOMAN CREDITED WITH
SAVING PARIS DURING TIMES OF CRISIS

French School (17th century): Geneviève in front of the Hôtel de Ville

Musée de la Ville de Paris / Musée Carnavalet, Paris, France

In mid-April 451, anxious inhabitants of the Ile de la Cité looked toward the Left Bank for a signal from Mount Leucotitius (the site of today's Panthéon). The mountain was the highest, most visible vantage point from which the government could quickly alert the whole city of unfolding events and approaching danger. Attila was slaughtering his way from Reims toward Paris, and a burning torch or fading light on the mountain would herald his defeat or approach. Some citizens had already loaded possessions into carts and headed south toward Orléans after messengers and spies reported that Attila had set his sights on Paris. They fled the *île* across its two bridges, the wooden Grand Pont (today's Pont Notre-Dame) and the Petit Pont (still known by the same name).

Geneviève, a Gallo-Roman noblewoman influential in city matters, pressed them not to leave. She warned that an abandoned city would be easy prey for the invaders and that children and elders would die in flight without food and shelter. Skeptical townspeople doubted her motives—she was a descendant of Frank "outsiders"—but the burning torch on Mount Leucotitius soon proved her right. Attila turned

south to the more desirable Orléans, and Geneviève's authority increased tenfold.

Intermittent waves of barbarian invasions had driven the people of Paris from former settlements on the Left Bank to safety inside fortified walls on the *île*. As a child, Geneviève saw boatloads of wounded Gallo-Roman soldiers ferried along the Seine to hospital barracks installed in what had been the Roman thermal baths (today's Cluny Museum) and forum.

In permanent transition, the city government restored deteriorating Roman buildings that littered the *île* and its surroundings. Among them were the Emperor Julian's praesidium (where the Conciergerie now stands), the Arènes de Lutèce amphitheater (today fully visible near rue Monge, its entrance is at rue de Navarre and rue des Arènes), the military encampment (Luxembourg Gardens), and aqueducts to the south and west.

The peace after Attila did not last long. In 464 King Childéric and his tribe, the Franks, besieged and conquered the city. This time benefiting from her Frankish origins, Geneviève helped negotiate the release of prisoners captured by Childéric—she, a Gallo-

eastern tip of the Cité, the Church of St. Etienne rose up like a phoenix from the ruins of Jupiter's temple (the church extended beyond the entrance to the north portal of today's Notre Dame Cathedral up to the plaque on the pavement marking its former location), and the Baptistry of Saint-Jean-en-Rond (a small separate chapel which stood next to the north wall of St. Etienne) replaced the crumbling altar to Mars.

The Catholic Church gained converts by merging the histories and attributes of pagan gods with those of Christian saints. To further the cause, Geneviève convinced priests to build a basilica over the tomb of St. Denis at the site of pagan rituals. The construction project unified a demoralized populace who for decades had seen their economy ruined and monuments toppled.

Clovis also broke ground on the Left Bank for a church. Following Frankish tradition, he stood facing west with his back to the old Roman forum (the area of the Sorbonne) and tossed the *francisque* (the Frankish war axe) to locate the spot. Land surveyors by his side plotted the 200- by 60-foot basilica that provided work for thousands of

Roman citizen, did not side with the Franks—and provisioned the starving citizens with grain she transported down the Seine from her family's farmlands in Meaux and Brie.

Geneviève was also a woman of the Church. When Clovis succeeded Childéric, she and Clovis's Catholic queen Clothilda converted him to their beliefs. Geneviève preached the gospel, healed the sick (some said miraculously), and coaxed the people to abandon their pagan practices. On the

artisans and builders. It crowned Mount Leucotitius near the former temple to the goddess Leucothea.

At Geneviève's death, Clovis and Clothilda buried her remains in that church (in the vicinity of today's Panthéon) which subsequently bore her name. Three centuries later the Abbey of St. Geneviève was constructed adjacent to it. Her relics increased the prestige of Paris, attracted large numbers of the faithful, and contributed to the local economy (pilgrims required food and lodging).

For centuries, during times of crisis or good fortune, elaborately staged processions wound their way from the abbey on what had come to be called the Montagne Sainte-Geneviève across the river to the parvis (square) Notre-Dame. In 1675, the chronicler Madame de Sévigné wrote:

Do you know how beautiful this procession is? All the monastic orders, all the parishes, all the shrines, all the priests of the parishes, all the canons of Notre Dame, along with Monsieur the Archbishop on foot pontifically blessing the people on the right and left all the way to the Cathedral. He blesses with the left hand while on his right it is the Abbot of Sainte-Geneviève, barefoot, with his cross and mitre, blessing modestly and devoutly, preceded by fifty friars, barefoot . . . Members of Parlement dressed in red robes and all the sovereign officials follow the shrine—which dazzles the eye with its precious stones—carried by twenty men, barefoot, garbed in white. . . . You will ask why they brought out her shrine; it was to stop the rains and bring on the warm weather. Both happened as soon as the procession was set in motion—as in general such benefits follow—and I think that it is to this that we owe the return of the King.[1]

By then Geneviève's life had become legend, and not by accident. Shortly after her death her Catholic biographer artfully fused the story of Geneviève's life with legends about the popular goddess Leucothea. Both the ancient city, Lutèce, and its mountain, Leucotitius, derive their names from their early protector. Sites all over Paris tell pieces of this story.

Sites

Panthéon
Place du Panthéon (5th arr.)
Métro: Cardinal Lemoine

The Place du Panthéon marks the site of two churches of St. Geneviève. The more recent one, the building that is now called the Panthéon, was built in 1764 by Louis XV, who named it the Church of Sainte-Geneviève because he sought the saint's help to cure an illness. Inside are murals of scenes from her life by Puvis de Chavannes (1824–1898).

The Lycée Henri IV just behind the Panthéon, at 23 rue Clovis, stands on the site of the earlier, medieval Church and Abbey of Sainte-Geneviève. In the school courtyard, accessible to the public, a wall from the abbey is still visible, as is the church belfry on rue Clovis.

Nineteenth-century excavations nearby revealed ruins of a Gallic temple that may have been dedicated to the cult of Leucothea. The proximity of Geneviève's basilica to the temple vestiges points to the Catholic Church's appropriation of this pagan site.

Across the street from the Lycée Henri IV, the Church of Saint-Etienne-du-Mont displays a relic, a finger bone, of Geneviève in her chapel on the right. The stained glass windows show her former basilica and scenes from her life as well as processions in her honor.

Pont de la Tournelle
(5th arr.)
Métro: Pont Marie

On this bridge, a slim white statue of Geneviève, her arm around a child, recalls her role in saving Paris from the Huns in 451 and supplying grain to its besieged citizens in 464. She faces east, the direction from which Attila's forces advanced and from which she transported the grain.

Cluny Museum
6, Place Paul Painlevé (5th arr.)
Tel: 01 53 73 78 16
Métro: Cluny or St. Michel
www.musee-moyenage.fr
Daily except Tuesday 9:15am to 5:45pm

The iconography of Leucothea and Geneviève portrays them both as protectors of sailors. A bas-relief of the goddess on a second-century Roman pillar, found on the Ile de la Cité, can be seen in the Roman Baths room. Sculpted on one facet of the pillar, she holds a torch and wears her identifying headband. Leucothea is credited with rescuing Odysseus from drowning; Geneviève's biography tells of a violent storm on the Seine during which she, like Leucothea, saved the sailors.

Notre Dame Cathedral

(4th arr.)
Tel: 01 42 34 56 10
Métro: Cité or St.-Michel/Notre-Dame
Cathedral: Daily 8am to 6:45pm
(Saturday and Sunday 7:15pm);
Reception: Monday to Friday 9:30am to
6pm (Saturday and Sunday 9am to 6pm)
Archaeological Crypt Museum: Daily
except Monday, 10am to 6pm.

Parvis Notre-Dame
On the right side of the Virgin (north) portal Geneviève stands holding a candle which the devil over her left shoulder snuffs out and the angel over her right reignites (a symbol of undying faith). The Christian candle replaced Leucothea's torch.

opposite: Statue of Geneviève in the Luxembourg gardens
Author photo

right: Goddess Leucothea on a pillar in the Roman baths room in the Musée de Cluny
Author photo

Geneviève's two-room house was located near this portal, as was the original, fourth-century Church of St. Etienne. In 528 Childebert, Clovis's son, built a new Church of St. Etienne next to it. Markings on the pavement for the sixth-century church can be found not far from the portal entry. Both churches were taken down in 1163 to make room for Notre Dame Cathedral.

above: Column capital in the Musée de Cluny from 12th century basilica of Saint Geneviève
Author photo

opposite: French School (16th century): Geneviève guarding her flock
Musée de la Ville de Paris / Musée Carnavalet, Paris, France

Archaeological Crypt Museum

It was a common belief that a saint worked miracles long after her death, like the miracle that occurred on November 3, 1130, when Geneviève was believed to have cured a hundred victims of ergot poisoning from moldy rye (known in French as *ardens* disease) during a procession of her relics in front of Notre Dame. To commemorate the event, the Church of Sainte-Geneviève-des-Ardens was built on the northwestern corner of the parvis, where it stood until 1747. It replaced the small sanctuary where her relics were stored during the ninth-century Norman invasions of Paris. The outline of the church is traced on the pavement directly above the Archaeological Crypt Museum where the foundations of the church are on display. The museum also contains the vestiges of the Gallo-Roman wall that surrounded the Ile de la Cité and the ruins of houses from the second to third centuries.

Church of Saint-Denys de la Chapelle

10, rue de la Chapelle (18th arr.)
Métro: Marx-Dormoy

Another mythic connection between Leucothea and Geneviève derives from the legend that the goddess had an adoptive son named Dionysios, the Greek name for Denis. St. Denis was the martyred bishop of Paris whose veneration Geneviève promoted by building a basilica dedicated to him. According to tradition, Saint-Denys de la Chapelle was originally a small chapel where Geneviève went to pray during the basilica's construction. The basilica was somewhere between Saint-Denys de la Chapelle and the later Basilica of Saint-Denis, north of Paris. The village of la Chapelle, in what is now the eighteenth arrondissement, derived its name from Geneviève's chapel.

❋ **Have a coffee at the Café aux Tours de Notre Dame on the corner of rue du Cloître Notre-Dame and rue d'Arcole, located next to the north tower of the cathedral, where Geneviève's small house stood.**

Héloïse

(D. 1164)
WOMAN OF LETTERS, PHILOSOPHER,
BIBLICAL SCHOLAR, "ABBESS OF GREAT
RENOWN"

In 1116 Paris heard reports of a lay woman scholar who devoted herself to philosophy and letters, unusual for women outside convents and court life. Héloïse was in her early twenties and, by all accounts, brilliant.

So was her tutor, thirty-seven-year-old Pierre Abélard, the most famous philosopher in Paris. Abélard taught at the Notre Dame school and on the Montagne Sainte-Geneviève, where his lectures were known to draw as many as three thousand students.

Paris was undeniably *the* center of learning in Europe, despite the fact that it was filthy and its buildings were in deplorable condition, the result of the ravages of war and centuries of neglect. To the east, the porch of the old Notre Dame Cathedral faced the Merovingian Church of St. Etienne built five hundred years earlier (the markings are visible on the parvis in front of the north Virgin portal).

Héloïse lived just behind the cathedral in the Cloître Notre-Dame with her uncle, Fulbert, a canon who oversaw the cathedral school. As a child she had been educated by Benedictine nuns in the northwest Paris suburb of Argenteuil. (Aside from her mother's name, Hersende, nothing is known about her

parents.) At the richly endowed convent of St. Marie her studies in grammar, Scripture, the Church fathers, and classical writers such as Ovid and Lucan, stoked her later passion for philosophy and letters. A precocious student, she left Argenteuil in her late teens for Fulbert's home where he selected a tutor for her at the cathedral school, an unprecedented opportunity for a young woman in Paris since girls were given little more than early schooling. Abélard described his new student: "In looks she did not rank lowest, while in the extent of her learning she stood supreme."[1]

The Notre Dame school had faculties in theology, law, and the arts, whose courses included the trivium (grammar, rhetoric, and dialectics) and quadrivium (music, arithmetic, geometry, and astronomy), all taught in Latin (hence the name "Latin Quarter" on the Left Bank). Theology students lived in canons' houses in the walled-off Cloître Notre-Dame next to the cathedral. The influx of young men caused bedlam in the neighborhood, but students had to be tolerated for the economy's sake. Abélard had been one of them until he began sparring with dean Guillaume de Champeaux. Enthusiastic classmen packed in to watch the theological debates where Abélard refuted Champeaux's arguments with verve and panache, and not a little arrogance. Become persona non grata, he was dismissed from the school and crossed the Seine to lecture to students on the Left Bank Montagne-Sainte-Geneviève.

Translations of Greek philosophers sweeping across Europe had begun to chip away at medieval Christianity. Theology students, used to memorizing biblical passages with officially sanctioned interpretations (glosses), now called upon Aristotelian logic to pose questions about human experience, God, and the world.

The Church at the time governed every part of a person's life. From sunrise to sunset church bells in Paris rang out the periods of the day, not by hours but by prayers: *matins, lauds, prime, terce, sext, none (noon), vespers, compline.* A housewife's recipe called for simmering ingredients the time it took to say a *miserere* ("Out of the depths, I cry unto You, O Lord . . . ").

While Héloïse breathed the air of religion, she welcomed all studies that subjected traditional beliefs to a new kind of scrutiny. The few examples of her writing that have survived offer proof of her learnedness. In one short letter addressed to Abélard, allusions to writers abound as if they were common daily fare:

You travel with the wheels of the virtues [St. Jerome and Cicero], and for this reason you are far more precious to me than gold or topaz [Psalm 118, 127]. For I cannot deny myself to you any more than Byblis could to Caunus, or Oenone to Paris, or Briseis to Achilles [Ovid's Metamorphoses *and* Heroides*]. . . . What more? I send you as many joys as Antiphila had when she welcomed back Clinia [Terence's* Heautontimorumenos*]. . . . Live and be well, that you may see the time of Elijah [Malachi, Ecclesiasticus].*[2]

Abélard is not lighthearted when he writes to Héloïse:

I am inferior to you in every way, because you surpass me even where I seemed to surpass you. Your talent, your command of language, beyond your years and sex, is now beginning to extend itself into manly strength. . . . Do not people esteem you more than everybody else, do they not set you up on high, so that from there you can shine forth like a lamp and be observed by all?[3]

With both intellectual compatibility and erotic attraction between student and teacher, Héloïse and Abélard's lessons soon became a blend of philosophy and passionate lovemaking. Héloïse never considered their affair sinful. Well versed in the classical writers, she considered her bond with Abélard to be like Cicero's understanding of friendship:

You know, my heart's love, that the services of true love are properly fulfilled only when they are continually owed, in such a way that we act for a friend according to our strength and not stop wishing to go beyond our strength.[4]

Abélard did share her view but later confessed to less noble drives.

For a few months Fulbert knew nothing, even though Abélard lived under his roof and students in the streets were singing Abélard's love songs. Héloïse later wrote to Abélard:

. . . [Y]ou left many love-songs and verses which won wide popularity for the charm of their words and tunes and kept your name continually on everyone's lips. The beauty of the airs ensured that even the unlettered did not forget you; more than anything this

made women sigh for love of you. And as most of the songs told of our love, they soon made me widely known and roused the envy of many women against me.[5]

When Fulbert discovered the truth, he insisted they marry. Héloïse refused, even after giving birth to their son Astrolabe (who was raised in Brittany), stubbornly citing St. Jerome's argument against marriage, whose binding attachments encumbered the spirit. She believed that the love she shared with Abélard transcended hollow conventions and worried that the cares of domestic life would ruin his reputation —marriage was considered unmanly for a philosopher. For a while the two were separated, but corresponded clandestinely.

Finally, Héloïse and Abélard appeased Fulbert and married but asked that the nuptials be kept secret. Despite their wishes, Fulbert broadcast their marriage, prompting Héloïse subsequently to deny it. Unyielding in her decision to protect Abélard's stature and confident in the higher union she enjoyed with him, she insisted on continuing to live in her uncle's house as a single woman. Seething with anger, Fulbert plotted his revenge.

In medieval Paris, people believed the night belonged to Satan. When the last church bells sounded, the dark, narrow streets were avoided for their mischief and crime. Into the obscurity Fulbert sent hired men to castrate Abélard in his bed. Abélard wrote:

Next morning the whole city gathered before my house and the scene of horror and amazement, mingled with lamentations, cries and groans which exasperated and distressed me, is difficult, no, impossible, to describe. In particular, the clerks and, most of all, my pupils tormented me with their unbearable weeping and wailing until I suffered more from their sympathy than from the pain of my wound, and felt the misery of my mutilation less than my shame and humiliation.[6]

Soon after the assault Abélard made the shocking decision that he and Héloïse would enter the Benedictine order, she in the Argenteuil suburb, and he at the Abbey of St. Denis to the north of Paris. Husband and wife did not meet again until nine years later when Abbot Suger of St. Denis reclaimed Héloïse's St. Marie convent for his monks and expelled her religious community (an arched bas-relief, thought to be from her convent, is in

the Cluny Museum). By then Héloïse had become prioress and was responsible for the nuns. Abélard, although poor and censured for works declared heretical, gave them his primitive, thatched oratory in Nogent-sur-Seine, south of Paris.

Four years after Héloïse's nuns moved to his oratory Abélard wrote a confessional biography, hoping to regain his teaching post in Paris. When his autobiographical *Historia Calamitatum* (Story of My Calamitous Life*)* fell into Abbess Héloïse's hands, she wrote to reprove him for his long neglect:

You know, beloved, as the whole world knows, how much I have lost in you, how at one wretched stroke of fortune that supreme act of flagrant treachery robbed me of my very self in robbing me of you. . . . [I]mmediately at your bidding I changed my clothing along with my mind, in order to prove you the sole possessor of my body and my will alike... It was not any sense of vocation which brought me as a young girl to accept the austerities of the cloister, but your bidding alone, and if I deserve no gratitude from you, you may judge for yourself how my labours are in vain. I can expect no reward for this from God, for it is certain that I have done nothing as yet for love of him. . . . I would have had no hesitation, God knows, in following you or going ahead at your bidding to the flames of Hell. . . .[7]

A series of letters between them followed in which they made peace with each other and their lives in religion.

(Until 1999 only three letters in Héloïse's hand were known to exist and for centuries their authenticity had been challenged, some scholars claiming that Héloïse could never have composed the sophisticated arguments they contained. A cache of their love letters, recently surfaced in Burgundy, reveals a fully-realized Héloïse: lover, philosopher, biblical scholar, and poet.)

In the meantime, Abbess Héloïse began to transform the oratory in Nogent-sur-Seine into one of the richest, most highly esteemed convents in France, visited by royalty, bishops, and abbots. A scholar who knew Greek, Latin, and Hebrew, she instructed her nuns in Scripture and the sacred texts.

In 1143 when Peter the Venerable, abbot of the great Cluny Abbey in Burgundy, wrote Héloïse to inform her about Abélard's final days there, he took the opportunity to praise her for her intellect and piety:

I had not yet quite passed the bounds of youth and reached early manhood when I knew of your name and your reputation, not yet for religion but for your virtuous and praiseworthy studies. I used to hear at that time of the woman who although still caught up in the obligations of the world, devoted all her application to knowledge of letters, something which is very rare, and to the pursuit of secular learning. . . . It would also be pleasant for me to talk with you like this for longer, both because I am delighted by your renowned learning, and far more because I am drawn to you by what many have told me about your religion. If only our Cluny possessed you, or you were confined in the delightful prison of Marcigny [a Cluniac convent] with other handmaids of Christ [nuns] who are there awaiting their freedom in heaven! I would have preferred your wealth of religion and learning to the richest treasures of any kings, and would rejoice to see that noble community of sisters still further illuminated by your presence there.[8]

Sites

Site of the Cloître Notre-Dame
Area between rue du Cloître Notre-Dame and the Quai aux Fleurs
Ile de la Cité (4th arr.)
Métro: Cité

The *cloître* (cloister, an enclosed area) had three gates which opened into a sumptuous complex of gardens and houses between these two streets. Héloïse and Abélard's residence (see below) was in this complex.

On the north face of Notre Dame near the corner of rue du Cloître Notre-Dame and rue Massillon are seven bas-reliefs from the beginning of the thirteenth century which relate events in the life of Mary: her death, burial, resurrection, and so on. Given their location, inside the enclosure of the cloister, these probably were meant to instruct pupils at the Cathedral School. The red door further along was the entry into the Cathedral from the cloister for the canons and pupils.

Fulbert's house (residence of Héloïse and Abélard)

9 and 11, Quai aux Fleurs (4th arr.)
Métro: Cité

In 1118, Abélard lived on this site under Fulbert's roof as Héloïse's tutor. In the nineteenth century there was a resurgence of interest in medieval life in Paris and the lovers' story became well-known. In 1817, the house (rebuilt in 1849) became a pilgrimage site, along with Héloïse and Abélard's grave in Père Lachaise, one of the most visited today.

Conciergerie

2, boulevard du Palais (1st arr.)
Tel: 01 53 40 60 80
Métro: Cité or St. Michel
Daily 9:30am to 6pm, November–February 9am to 5pm

The Conciergerie was built on the vestiges of what had been the Royal Palace from the tenth to the fourteenth centuries, before Philippe Auguste's construction of the Louvre. The main hall recalls its early origins, and in the Guard's Room one of the column capitals bears a bas-relief of Abélard and Héloïse, presumably an "indelicate" object of amusement for the guards: Héloïse is holding Abélard's severed member.

Gravesite

Division 7, Père Lachaise Cemetery (20th arr.)
Principal entry: 16, rue de Repos
Tel: 01 40 71 75 60
Métro: Philippe Auguste
Generally the cemetery is open Monday–Friday 7:30am to 6pm; Saturday 8:30am to 6pm; Sunday 9am–6pm, 5:30pm November–March, but hours may vary.
www.pere-lachaise.com

Basilica of St. Denis

2, rue de Strasbourg
Place de l'Hôtel-de-Ville, St. Denis
Métro: Strasbourg–St. Denis

Suger was the abbot of this prestigious monastery (destroyed during the Revolution and rebuilt by Viollet-le-Duc under Napoleon III, now a monument of France) where Abélard entered the Benedictine order around 1119. As such, Suger had authority over other Benedictine houses. In 1128 he falsely accused Héloïse's religious order at St. Marie in Argenteuil and nuns in other communities of immoral behavior as a pretext to reclaim for the monks convents of the abbey which had been run by women for centuries.

The Gothic Abbey and Basilica of St. Denis (open to the public) houses the remains of all but three monarchs from the tenth century to the Revolution.

❋ Restaurant Au Vieux Paris d'Arcole

24, rue Chanoinesse (4th arr.)
Tel: 01 40 51 78 52
Métro: Cité
www.auvieuxparis.fr
Noon–2pm and 6:30–10:30pm, closed for lunch Monday and Saturday

The restaurant is in the former home of a canon of Notre Dame, built in 1512 near the site of Héloïse's house. The building, its location, and the fresh, organic produce delivered directly from the owner's farms recreate the ambiance of dining in the sixteenth-century enclosure of the Cloître Notre-Dame.

❋ *The Letters of Abelard and Heloise*

Translated by Betty Radice, Penguin, London, 2004.

For readers wanting to read the letters and Abélard's *My Calamitous Life.*

Constant J. Mews: *The Lost Love Letters of Heloise and Abelard,*

New York, Palgrave Macmillan, 2008.

The detective-like story of scholar Constant J. Mews's recent discovery of the lost love letters of Abélard and Héloïse, and the love letters themselves.

Alexandre Marie Lenoir: The tomb of Abélard and Héloïse

Christine de Pizan

(1364–1431?)

FIRST PROFESSIONAL WOMAN WRITER IN
FRANCE, BOOKMAKER, AND APOLOGIST
FOR WOMEN

Christine de Pizan: Christine de Pizan stepped into a scribe's shop on the rue des Ecrivains and handed the man at the desk her manuscript. She wanted the pages ruled and the text copied in large Gothic script, leaving space for the images to be added by artisans. The copyist was puzzled: "Madame, it is inappropriate for a woman to be learned, as it is so rare." "Sir," she replied, "it is even less fitting for a man to be ignorant, as it is so common."[1]

She had begun writing when her husband died suddenly in 1389. Widowed at twenty-five with three children, a niece, and a mother to provide for, she decided to take up her pen. Writing was an unlikely profession for a woman who grew up at Court (her father was counselor to King Charles V) and whose husband had been Secretary to King Charles VI. "Ladies" like her did not write to earn a living, and before she could do so, she would need time to brush up on her studies. As a child she had been tutored in French, Italian, and Latin texts, but since her marriage at fifteen she had devoted herself to

children, not books. In her autobiography she describes her self-designed course of study:

I began with the ancient histories from the beginnings of the world, then the history of the Hebrews, the Assyrians, and the early kingdoms, proceeding from one to the other and coming to the Romans, the French, the Britons, and several other historians, and then to what scientific learning I was able to grasp in the time available for study.

Next, I took up the works of the poets, my knowledge increasing all the while. I was glad to find in them a style that seemed natural to me, and took pleasure in their subtle allegories and lovely material hidden beneath delightful moral fictions, as well as the beautiful forms of their verse and prose adorned with polished rhetoric, subtle language, and piquant proverbs. . . . Thus I began to write short pieces in a lighter vein, and like the workman who perfects his technique by practicing, I learned more and more new things through the study of diverse disciplines, and refined my style with greater subtleness and the use of nobler material.[2]

French School (15th century): Christine de Pizan writing at her desk, from *The Works of Christine de Pisan*

French School (15th Century): Christine de Pizan's Barbeau tower (far left), Charles VI's Hôtel Saint-Paul, and the Bastille

Archives, Musée de la Ville de Paris / Musée Carnavalet, Paris, France

Fortunately for Pizan, the city at that time was rife with opportunity for the talented.

Fifteenth-century Paris was a thriving center of book production: histories, romances, prayer books, Ovid's *Metamorphoses*, the lives of the saints, and more. The highest-quality manuscripts were prized by King Charles VI, the dukes of Burgundy and of Orléans, and others at Court. Commissions drew artisans from all over Europe while French illuminators traveled to Italy to copy the styles of acknowledged masters Simone Martini and Pietro Lorenzetti. Master illuminator Jacquemart de Hesdin also brought back secret recipes for new pigments. In Paris, pigment ingredients were sold by alchemists on the rue Neuve Notre-Dame (the name of this vanished street is marked on the parvis Notre Dame pavement in front of the Cathedral).

For luxury manuscripts like the *Très Riches Heures* commissioned by the Duc Jean de Berry, illuminators ground lapis lazuli from Afghanistan or extracted red from heated minium (lead oxide), hence the name *miniatures*, and mixed them with a binding agent or glue to adhere to parchment. They applied thin sheets of gold leaf with a tweezer-shaped tool after running it through their oily hair (to prevent static), then buffed the gold with a hound's tooth.

In Pizan's best-known work, *The Book of the City of Ladies*, she singled out one such artist, the illustrator of several of her books:

I know a woman today, named Anastasie, who is so learned and skilled in painting manuscript borders and miniature backgrounds that one cannot find an artisan in all the city of Paris—where the best in the world are found—who can surpass her, nor who can paint flowers and details as delicately as she does, nor whose work is more highly esteemed, no matter how rich or precious the book is. People cannot stop talking about her. And I know from experience, for she has executed several things for me which stand out among the ornamental borders of the great masters.[3]

Anastasie, about whom little is known, probably worked in a Left Bank atelier like the one on rue des Enlumineurs (today rue Boutebrie) which opened onto the nine-foot-wide street. Artisans needed light but no wind if laying gold leaf or powder. The rest of the house would have been living space: a small kitchen in back and bedrooms on three floors above for family or hired journeymen. The tall, gabled houses stood chock-a-block next to the Church of St. Severin. Pizan knew the neighborhood well.

She had all the right connections for a writer and bookmaker. Having mingled with royalty and being of Italian heritage, she collaborated on French translations of Boccaccio and was well acquainted with Giacomo and Dino Rapondi, Italian merchants in the rue des Lombards (still near the Church of St. Merri in the 4th arrondissement), who financed book production for well-to-do customers. Though Henri Luilier, across from the old Royal Palace (now the Palais de Justice), was the largest bookseller in town, the Court had personal *valets de chambre* who ordered books for Charles VI and knew the Italianate taste of Jean de Berry. In 1404 Philippe de Bourgogne asked Pizan to write a biography of his brother Charles V, a king she had known and loved as a child.

It was a prestigious commission. To do research she climbed the winding, dank steps in the Louvre to Charles V's library tower, later writing, "I gathered my information concerning his life, surroundings, behavior, life-style, and his specific acts either from chronicles or from talking to famous people who are still alive." She was thus able to include in her account of his life details of his daily routine:

This king kept in his chapel a lighted candle, which was divided into twenty-four parts: eight of these the king devoted to prayers and study, eight more to tending to the needs of his kingdom and the other eight to personal recreation [an irony that the king known for the fourteenth-century clock on the Cité Palais ordered his day by candle notches].[4]

Pizan produced, on average, one book a year, correcting the copyist's text and discussing layouts with master illuminators. She had already written books about court life and collections of ballads for the dukes and king and queen.

A paramount theme was her defense of women. In a bestseller of the time, *The Romance of the Rose,* university professor Jean de Meung had accused women of all the evils visited upon men. In her *Treatise on The Romance of the Rose* Pizan cited passage after passage to discredit his rants as baseless and defamatory. If women are so pernicious, she asks:

I beg all those who claim him [Meung] as their authority and lend him their faith to please inform me how many men have they have seen accused, killed, hanged, or blamed in the streets on accusation by their wives? . . . [W]here are the lands and countries which were lost through their misdeeds? . . . And how can they deceive you? If they ask for money from your purse, then they neither steal it nor carry it off: don't give it to them if that is what you want. And if you say that you are besotted by them, then you need not be so stupid. Do they go looking for you in your homes, begging your favor or taking you by force?

Pizan concluded that Meung's book was "an indoctrination in deceit . . . a universal libel."[5]

When the Sorbonne professors demanded an apology for an attack on one of their own, the controversy spiraled into a spate of letters between outraged university men and Pizan's supporters at Court. Unfazed, and as if to drive home her point, she produced a feminist utopia extolling great women and heroines throughout history.

It was called *The Book of the City of Ladies.* The narrative follows three Ladies named Reason, Justice, and Rectitude, as they build a city to protect women who, living under the governance of men, have been ravished by war and the ills of social upheaval. In her figurative city (the book itself) Pizan gathers a cavalcade of women and tells the stories of their accomplishments: saints, queens, warriors, ordinary women of integrity and intelligence, cultural innovators who advanced the causes of their people—such as Saint Lucy, the biblical Esther, warrior Penthesilea, and the poet Sappho, to name a few.

Pizan constructs the city of extraordinary women, she writes, because, "judging from the treatises of all philosophers and poets and from all orators . . .

[t]hey all concur in one conclusion: that the behavior of women is inclined to and full of every vice." Astonishing for a Catholic woman, Pizan then holds God accountable for having created women "inferior." She claims not to understand God's unfairness and concludes that she is less obliged to serve him than man is:

Alas, God, why did You not let me be born in the world as a man, so that all my inclinations would serve You better, and so that I would not stray in anything, and would be as perfect as a man is said to be? But since Your kindness has not been extended to me, then forgive my negligence in Your service, most fair Lord, and may it not displease You, for the servant who receives fewer gifts from his lord is less obliged in his service.[6]

If Pizan wanted to restore forgotten models of women and emphasize civilian suffering under the stewardship of men, her critique could not have been more timely.

In Paris the social and political systems were crumbling around her. The first cracks appeared in the spring of 1392 with King Charles VI's episode of dementia during a hunting trip. When the disorder recurred more and more frequently, Charles VI's brother Louis d'Orléans and cousin Jean de Bourgogne began to vie for control of the crown. Bourgogne assassinated Orléans in 1407 (a wooden historic marker indicates where he was murdered on rue des Francs-Bourgeois to the east of rue du Temple) setting off a civil war from 1410 to 1419. The Armagnacs (Orléans's faction) and Burgundians (Bourgogne's followers) alternately occupied the city, massacred the others' partisans, and set fire to homes and institutions.

Pizan's pen tracked one disaster after another with books on chivalry and warfare, the body politic, and lamentations for France.

In 1418 she stopped inveighing against the madness around her and retired to the Abbey of Saint-Louis in Poissy. As patronage of the arts waned in Paris due to the devastation of the economy, artists emigrated elsewhere, and houses on rue des Enlumineurs stood empty. But in 1429 a surprise event moved Pizan to write one last poem, an elegy to a strange young woman who led an attack on Burgundian Paris in the hopes that the Armagnac supporters of Charles VII would rise up against the Burgundian occupation. To Pizan the heroine seemed to have emerged from her own *Book of the City of Ladies.* Her name was Joan of Arc.

Sites

Site of Tour Barbeau
32, Quai des Célestins (4th arr.)
Métro: Pont Marie
Christine de Pizan's residence, a police station today, was located here. It joined the Philippe Auguste wall to the new 1380 Charles V wall that encompassed the Bastille.

Site of Charles V's Hôtel Saint-Paul
From Quai des Célestins to rue Saint-Antoine and from rue des Jardins Saint-Paul to rue Beautrellis (4th arr.)
Métro: St. Paul, Pont Marie
Charles V conducted affairs at the Louvre (the old fortress built by Philippe Auguste in 1200), but moved his residence to the Hôtel Saint-Paul in the Marais. By Charles V's time, the Right Bank had become the commercial district: He built new walls beyond the twelfth-century *enceinte* of Philippe Auguste that connected his *hôtel* with the Bastille fortress.

The street names in the area occupied by Charles's *hôtel* recall the monarch, his gardens, and menagerie: rue Charles V, rue des Jardins Saint-Paul, rue Beautrellis (beautiful trellis), rue des Lions. Courtyards and shops within this block of streets give an idea of the expanse of Charles V's, and later Charles VI's, court residence.

Philippe Auguste wall
Lycée Charlemagne
14, rue Charlemagne (4th arr.)
Métro: Pont Marie
A remaining section of the twelfth-century Philippe Auguste wall is in full view on the west side of the rue des Jardins Saint-Paul. The wall is attached to the Lycée Charlemagne.

Musée du Louvre
(1st arr.)
Tel: 01 40 20 50 50
Métro: Louvre-Rivoli
Daily except Tuesday 9am to 6pm;
Wednesday, Friday until 10pm
www.louvre.fr

Sully Wing
Just inside the Sully entrance, on the right, are vestiges of the stairs that Pizan climbed to Charles V's library tower. In 1367, it was here that Charles V arranged his books. The first-floor walls were paneled with wood from Ireland; the vaulted ceiling, with

cypress. Each entry door was seven feet high by three wide, and "the thickness of three fingers." All the windows were covered with brass wire trellises "for protection from birds and other animals."

Richelieu Wing
First room of the French Paintings Section

In this section of French Paintings from the Middle Ages is a large mural in grisaille (gray tones) of the Crucifixion, by the famous illuminator, the Parement Master. Patrons King Charles V and Jean de Bourbon, whom Pizan knew at Court, are depicted kneeling.

On the opposite wall, in the case, is a painting of Christ carrying the cross by Jacquemart de Hesdin. Pizan's illuminators were probably trained in Jacquemart's workshop.

Tour Jean sans Peur Museum (Tower of John the Fearless of Burgundy)

20, rue Etienne Marcel (2nd arr.)
Tel: 01 40 26 20 28
Métro: Etienne Marcel
www.tourjeansanspeur.com
Wednesday–Sunday 1:30 to 6pm;
November 12–April 10 open Wednesday, Saturday, Sunday only

This is the restored tower of the Duke of Burgundy's Hôtel d'Artois. The opening page of Christine de Pizan's *Mutation of Fortune* shows her presenting her book to Jean de Bourgogne, in his tower room.

Rue de la Parcheminerie and rue Boutebrie

(5th arr.)
Métro: Cluny

Illuminator and copyist ateliers had been located in these two streets since 1292, when rue de la Parcheminerie (parchment) was rue des Ecrivains (writers) and rue Boutebrie was rue des Enlumineurs (illuminators).

❋ *Henry V*

Director: Laurence Olivier
Cast: Laurence Olivier, Robert Newton, Leslie Banks
Two Cities Films, 1944

In this film version of Shakespeare's play, Olivier uses reproductions of the famous Berry illuminations (*Les Très Riches Heures du duc de Berry*) as a background. The details show Charles VI's court (even Berry's pug nose is visible), peasants warming themselves by the fire, and the Agincourt battle in 1415 when the English defeated the French.

❋ **L'Auberge Nicholas Flamel**

51, rue de Montmorency (3rd arr.)
Tel: 01 42 71 77 78
Métro: Rambuteau or Arts et Métiers
www.auberge-nicolas-flamel.fr
Monday through Saturday, noon to 2:30 and 7pm to 10:30pm. Sunday by reservation only.
Closed Sunday, three weeks in August

Nicholas Flamel came to Paris from Pontoise to work as a copyist and bookseller. He changed his mind when a foreign bookseller sold him a manuscript which supposedly contained the secret of the philosopher's stone. He claimed the secret enabled him to turn lead into gold which made him and his wife, Dame Pernelle, rich. They then financed fourteen hospitals, seven churches, and several houses. This one they built in 1407 as a refuge for the homeless.

The restaurant's menu offers traditional French cuisine. The original stone walls and exposed beams are reminiscent of Christine de Pizan's era.

A tower room in the Hôtel d'Artois where Christine de Pizan presented her books to the Duc de Bourgogne
Author photo

Marie de Rabutin-Chantal, Marquise de Sévigné

(1626–1696)

WOMAN OF LETTERS, *SALONNIÈRE*, AND
CHRONICLER OF PARISIAN LIFE AND
LOUIS XIV'S COURT

Claude Lefebvre: Portrait of Marie de Rabutin-Chantal, Madame de Sevigné

Musée de la Ville de Paris / Musée Carnavalet, Paris, France / Giraudon / The Bridgeman Art Library International

It was with both dread and relief that Madame de Sévigné stepped down from her carriage at rue des Lions in the Marais in the fall of 1651, arriving from her estate in Brittany, her son and daughter trailing behind. Her dissolute husband had again humiliated her in Paris, this time with his ignominious death in a duel over a courtesan.

The fashionable Marais had always been her neighborhood. From the elegant town house on the Place des Vosges, where she was born, to the home of her Coulanges relatives on rue des Francs-Bourgeois where she moved after her parents' death, she knew the *quartier* well. Growing up in the company of her cousins was a soothing balm to parental loss at seven, but equally important was the companionship of another uncle who lived on the Place des Vosges, the Archbishop of Bourges, a man whose library provided her with an infinite supply of books during her adolescent years.

The deaths of her mother and father may have taught her the fragile nature of family ties, but marriage introduced her to the harsh realities of aristocratic womanhood. In 1644 she married the Marquis de Sévigné, a Breton noble with little to recommend him: no position at court or in the military. Like most marriages of this sort, neither the bride nor groom had a say in the choice of spouse; the contract was arranged solely with finances in mind. Her husband proved to be a rake of the first order, settling his young family in his estate in Brittany, to return alone to his bachelor life in Paris. Later Madame de Sévigné wrote about the year of her husband's death, 1651, as a time of liberation:

At first the only dates outstanding in my memory were the years of my birth and marriage, but now I prefer to forget the year of my birth, which saddens and depresses me, and to substitute the year of my widowhood, which was peaceful, somewhat happy, and blessedly ordinary, out of the public eye.[1]

Widowhood at twenty-five granted her an independence that she would never again have to surrender to a man. As she said, "Young widows are not to be pitied; they will delight in being their own mistresses or changing masters."[2]

More important to the Marquise than prospective husbands was her daughter, Françoise-Marguerite. When Françoise's husband became the Count of Grignon, Governor of Provence, Sévigné wrote her almost daily letters chronicling events in Paris. (Almost a thousand letters to her daughter, some as long as twenty-six pages, have survived.) Some dealt with domestic concerns like the one of October 7, 1677, which described the new home Sévigné had just leased in the Marais, the Hôtel Carnavalet:

It's an excellent deal: it will suit us all and quite handsomely. Since one cannot have everything, we will have to do without the parquet floors and small fireplaces that are in vogue now, but we will have an attractive courtyard, a beautiful garden, and a fashionable neighborhood.[3]

Other letters kept Françoise current on news Sévigné culled in the salons of her friends—Catherine de Rambouillet, Madeleine de Scudéry, Françoise

Scarron—and during her attendance at Court.

Madame de Sévigné was not a professional writer; she never aspired to earn her living by the pen. The literary phenomenon she became was simply a case of true talent rising to the surface. Friends and family could not resist circulating her letters for their good read and newsy content.

What they loved was the immediacy of her reports. In July 1676 she was in the crowd near Notre Dame to give an eyewitness account of the execution of the infamous murderer, the Marquise de Brinvilliers, who poisoned hapless victims, including hospital patients at the Hôtel Dieu, who she used as guinea pigs for her deadly concoctions, the ultimate purpose of which was to do away with her brothers, husband, and father:

At last, it is over, La Brinvilliers has gone up in smoke: her poor, little body has been cast, after execution, into a roaring fire and her ashes scattered to the wind; so that now we are inhaling her, and we wonder how her airborne little spirits might poison our own humor.[4]

Brinvilliers's crimes were but the tip of the iceberg of what became known

as the *affaire des poisons.* Another notorious criminal, a certain Catherine Montvoisin, called "La Voisin," had been executed for conducting satanic rites with the blood of fetuses she had aborted for the purpose of making "magical potions." In 1682 even Louis XIV's mistress Madame de Montespan was implicated; she had allegedly engaged La Voisin to obtain "fluids" for an aphrodisiac to mix with the king's food to restore Montespan to his favor after another courtesan had caught his eye. In all, 147 prisoners were locked up in the Bastille and Vincennes for charges of having acquired poison recipes with the intent to commit murder. Among them were many a woman of noble rank who had rid herself of an unwanted husband.

Marriage, which the Marquise de Sévigné called slavery, was a contentious topic in salons and at Court where two of her close friends provoked discussion of the matter. Novelist Madame de Lafayette wrote *The Princess of Clèves* (modeled after Sévigné) in which the happy ending was the independence of widowhood, not the slavery of marriage. And when Madeleine de Scudéry's novels granted female characters the freedom to marry whom they pleased or to not marry at all, Boileau, Louis XIV's historiographer, accused Scudéry of inciting immoral behavior and endangering the nation; Louis needed revenues from nobles' estates and if women married "down" for love, not property, the revenues would be lost.

Madame de Sévigné, a frequent guest at Court, kept her daughter abreast of discussions and developments there. Reporting on delicate matters involving the king and his mistresses, she used code names to describe the dilemma of Madame de Montespan, who had been Louis's longtime favorite:

Everyone thinks that the Friend [Louis] is out of love and that Quanto [Mme de Montespan] is in a quandary between the consequences of granting the king her favors [she had already given birth to seven royal bastards], or the danger of witholding them, for fear that he would seek them elsewhere.[5]

Mistresses were in more abundant supply than good *maîtres d'hôtel* (master headwaiters), the loss of whom chagrined Louis deeply. In April 1671 Madame de Sévigné sent word of François Vatel's demise at the King's feast at Chantilly:

I have just heard the news that Vatel, the great Vatel, maître d'hôtel of M Fouquet and Monsieur le Prince, this man so distinguished among others, whose head was capable of handling all the affairs of State; this man whom I knew, who having seen at eight o'clock this morning that his order of seafood had not yet arrived, could not suffer the disgrace he knew would follow, and in a word, he ran himself through on his poniard. You can imagine the upset that such a tragic accident caused during this royal feast. And to think that the shipment arrived just as he was expiring.[6]

On January 3, 1689, Sévigné paints an irreverent picture of chivalry at the New Year's investiture of the marshals at Versailles. They appeared before the King,

. . . the maréchal de Bellefonds totally ridiculous, because by modesty and indifference, he had neglected to attach his hosiery ribbons so that he was half in the nude. The whole troop was magnificent, M. de la Trousse among the best: he had a problem with his wig that hung to the side then too far back making one cheek jut out. . . . But, along the same line, M. de Montchevreuil and M. de Villars got hooked onto each other with such a fury, the swords, the ribbons, the lace, all the trumpery, got so twisted together, entwined, cumbersome, all the little catches, so perfectly interwoven, that no one could separate them: the more they tried, the more entangled they got like interlocking rings; finally the entire ceremony, all the reverential bows, the whole merry-go-round having come to a stop, someone had to wrench them apart with force and only the strongest could carry it off. . .[7]

But Court news was not just chivalry and spectacle. Construction work on the Versailles palace (Louis moved in in 1682) revealed its macabre underside:

The king wants to go to Versailles, but it seems that God is not willing because the buildings are in no state to receive him. This is so because of the prodigious mortality of workers who are carted off every night, like the wagonloads of corpses from the Hôtel-Dieu. They conceal this ghastly transport to not frighten off other workers . . .[8]

Though Sévigné's letter about this shocking practice escaped the King's notice — the mail was under surveillance — those she addressed to his Minister of Finance did not. In 1659 Louis XIV's Minister of Finance Nicolas Fouquet gave a spectacular fête at his new château at Vaux-le-Vicomte.

The king, in attendance with his retinue, could barely contain his outrage when he saw that his minister's château was grander than the Louvre or Fontainebleau, a crime for which Fouquet was eventually condemned for life to the pestilential Pignerol prison. The unproven charges were treason and misuse of his office. Sévigné was a close friend, perhaps even romantically involved (historians only speculate). Unfortunately for the Marquise, her letters to Fouquet were among his stash of mistresses' love letters confiscated by the authorities. When her letters were found in such disreputable company, she feared for her reputation and appealed for help to her friend the Marquis de Pomponne:

But what do you suppose to be the contents of those little coffers? Would you have ever thought that my poor little letters, full of news of the marriage of M. de la Trousse and of the affairs of his household, would be so mysteriously filed? . . . I would be uneasy to have to justify myself, and perhaps uselessly, in the eyes of a thousand people who will never be convinced of the truth [that hers were not love letters]. I think that you understand how this pains someone like myself. I beg you to speak out on my behalf;

I cannot have enough friends at a time like this.[9]

Two separate authorites gave conflicting reports on the contents of the coffer: the King was quoted as having said that no letters from her were found, but the Secretary of State Le Tellier said there were indeed letters, but of an innocent nature. Madame de Sévigné was guarded by her good name, but in an absolute monarchy, it was not unreasonable to worry about worse consequences.

Madame de Sévigné was not used to having to defend the content of her letters. If anything, she feared the outcome of public attention, as she wrote to her daughter Françoise:

You praise my letters so far beyond their merit that if I were not sure that you would never again leaf through or reread them, I would fear suddenly to see myself in print by the betrayal of one of my friends.[10]

Madame de Sévigné wrote these words to her daughter six years before her death. The "treachery" she feared, but never lived to see—a first edition of her letters published in 1726—elevated her epistolary voice to the rank of national treasure. For biographers and

historians her correspondence remains a rich source of information about seventeenth-century Paris, reason enough for city officials to have housed the Museum of the History of Paris in her former residence, the Hôtel Carnavalet. Though she hardly hid her lamp under a bushel, she would never have expected to stand out herself as a memorable figure in history and literature.

Sites

Musée Carnavalet

23, rue de Sévigné (3rd arr.)
Tel: 01 44 59 58 58
Métro: St. Paul
Entrance: free
Daily except Monday 10am to 6pm
www.carnavalet.paris.fr

Mme de Sévigné was delighted to rent the Hôtel Carnavalet with its courtyard in front (where carriages pulled up to the entrance), and garden in back (so beautiful, she told her daughter, she would like to sleep there), the classic layout of *hôtels* of the period. Before she moved in, the Carnavalet had been recently renovated by François Mansart and the new sculptures of zodiac figures by Jean Goujon added in the courtyard. She took the rooms on the second floor and her family, when they visited, occupied the first and third floors. Her beloved uncle, the Abbé de Coulanges (whom she called Bien Bon and who had overseen her education as a child and would be a lifetime companion), had an entire wing to himself. There was a stable for eight horses and four carriages. Aside from the three portraits of her in the seventeenth-century room on the ground floor, nothing remains of her furnishings (which are found in her Brittany château, Les Rochers, near Rennes).

Birthplace
1 *bis*, Place des Vosges (3rd arr.)
Métro: St. Paul
The Place des Vosges, formerly Place Royale, was built in 1604 by Henri IV. The King and Queen Pavilions on the north and south of the square were surrounded by the thirty-five red brick buildings constructed over arcades. In the seventeenth century it was one of the most stylish neighborhoods in Paris. The house at 1 *bis*, marked by a plaque, belonged to Marie's maternal Coulanges family.

Hôtel de Coulanges
35–37, rue des Francs-Bourgeois (4th arr.)
Métro: St. Paul
This exquisite *hôtel* was acquired by Marie de Rabutin-Chantal's uncle, Philippe de Coulanges, in 1640. Marie lived here until her marriage in 1644.

 ### *Vatel*
Director: Roland Joffé
Cast: Gérard Depardieu, Uma Thurman, Tim Roth
Légende Entreprises, 2000

Le Roi danse (The King is Dancing)
Director: Gérard Corbiau
Cast: Benoît Magimel
K-Star, 2000
An elaborate costume drama of the rise of King Louis XIV to the peak of his power.

Garden of the Hôtel de Carnavalet
Author photo

Françoise d'Aubigné, Madame de Maintenon

(1635-1719)

SALONNIÈRE WHO BECAME MORGANATIC QUEEN OF LOUIS XIV

At a salon gathering in the Marais in 1666, Françoise Scarron was the cause of an outburst of uproarious laughter. When the young widow asked astrologer Barbé about her future, he told her a king would love her and she would reign.

An absurd prediction for a woman who was downright poor. Born to parents in a Niort debtors' prison and brought to Paris by her guardian, Françoise d'Aubigné faced two choices at sixteen: to enter the convent or marry Paul Scarron, a crippled but spirited star of literary salons nearly three times her senior, whose rheumatoid arthritis had contorted his body into a knot. To marry Scarron was preferable, having just escaped the tyranny of the Ursuline nuns on rue Saint-Jacques, where she had pleaded with her aunt for release from what she said was a hellish existence at the so-called house of God. But after she married Scarron, she found that nursing a paralytic husband, however talented, made for a dreary existence.

Dreary except for pleasurable interludes like the August day in 1660 when she watched from a window, in total rapture, Louis XIV's royal entry into the city along the rue Saint-Antoine with his bride Marie-Thérèse. (For centuries kings escorted their new queens into Paris through the Porte Saint-Antoine.) He rode with grace and surprising majesty. Believing she had never seen so handsome a man, she surmised that the queen must have gone to bed a happy woman. Returning to Paul's bedside to nurse him in his suffering, if only for the two months that remained for him to live, broke the spell of her reveries.

Paul and Françoise had set up house in the Marais at 56, rue de Turenne, a home they called the Hôtel de l'Impécuniosité for the soirées they hosted without the funds to supply even the simplest dinner to their guests. The company and entertainment were exceptional; the guests brought the food and cared little about their hosts' modest means. During the eight years of their marriage, writers and chroniclers like Madeleine de Scudéry and the Marquise de Sévigné were regulars, along with *frondeurs* (nobles who revolted against the king around 1650). Paul was a popular poet with a gift for irony and burlesque; his young wife, a shy consort whose wit did not go unnoticed.

After Scarron's death in 1660 Françoise remained in the Marais. First, she retired to the convent of the Hospitalières de Notre-Dame on rue de Turenne, a shelter for poor girls and women supported by Queen Anne of Austria, Louis XIV's mother. Later, while working as a housekeeper in the Albret household, she was introduced to Madame de Montespan, a frequent guest at the Hôtel d'Albret (still standing at 31, rue des Francs-Bourgeois). It was a meeting of historic import. Montespan would soon become Louis's new mistress and draw Françoise into the royal orbit.

When Montespan became pregnant with Louis XIV's first child, she asked Françoise, whom she considered a discreet and loyal friend, to care for the infant. To Françoise, a young woman who herself had strong ambi-

tions, it was an odious job. She agreed to take on the responsibility, on the condition that the king ask her himself. Eventually a house was bought outside the city walls on rue de Vaugirard (now in the 6th arrondissement — the city boundaries have since expanded) where Louis's "natural" children were secretly housed. After Françoise dined with her one evening during the winter of 1673–1674, Madame de Sévigné wrote:

We found it amusing to drive Mme Scarron home at midnight all the way to the end of the faubourg St. Germain . . . almost to Vaugirard in the country: an exquisite and grand house where no one is admitted. There is a large garden, and pleasant, large apartments [rooms]. *She has a carriage, servants, and horses, and is dressed modestly and magnificently, like a woman who spends her time with people of quality. She is amiable, beautiful, and unpretentious; an engaging conversationalist. We rode home along streets lit by lanterns, safe from robbers.*[1]

Sévigné, like others, knew what Françoise Scarron's duties were, but with Louis's new mistresses — Mademoiselles de Fontanges and de la Vallière — entering the limelight, may not have known the impression the royal governess was making on the king each

time he dropped in to visit his children. Three years later Sévigné's letter to her daughter registered the fall and rise of Louis's favorites at court: "Everyone believes that Mme de Montespan's star is fading. There are tears, there is gloom, there is affected cheerfulness, there is sulking. In sum, my dear, it is all over."[2]

Desperate to restore her superior position, Madame de Montespan availed herself of the services of a certain Madame Montvoisin. Her daughter later described to a horrified police lieutenant a macabre ritual ordered by her mother in which, at Madame de Montespan's mass, the *abbé* drained the blood from a preterm infant, consecrated the blood with the host, finished saying the mass, and disemboweled the body. The following day the blood was put in a phial, and taken by Madame de Montespan. By the time this crime came to light, Louis's complicitous *officier de la bouche* (the royal food taster) had already on several occasions mixed the contents of the "love potion" into his food, perhaps the cause of Louis's gastric disorders, which had mystified his doctors. Though the subsequent depositions of those involved in the shady affair pointed to Montespan's guilt, Louis decided, with the advice of Françoise de Maintenon (the king had ennobled Scarron with lands and a title), to let her remain at Versailles in smaller *apartments* rather than subject her to the humiliation of banishment, an outright confirmation of her crimes. It was Madame de Maintenon who delivered the news to Montespan that her relationship with the king was over, a bitter pronouncement from the woman who quietly, behind the scenes, had become her rival.

Toward the end of June 1680, Sévigné relayed more developments about Françoise de Maintenon:

They write me that the conversations between His Majesty and Mme de Maintenon grow longer and more engrossing . . . that the daughter-in-law [the Dauphine] sometimes pays them brief visits; that she finds them each seated in a large chair and that after her visit they resume the thread of their conversation. My friend tells me that no one approaches the lady without fear and respect and that the [King's] ministers pay her court the way others do to them [the ministers].[3]

Madame de Maintenon had become companion and advisor to the king. She sat off in the corner of the room during meetings about state affairs among him and his ministers, nodding or smiling in agreement. In private the conversations between her and Louis lasted for hours, after which the Abbé de Choisy even credited Madame de Maintenon with bringing Louis back to the communion table—previously he could not approach it during his adulterous affairs with mistresses. To Choisy the king's apparently chaste relationship with Maintenon allowed him to do so.

But these long tête-à-têtes with an attractive king did not preclude her own temptations or his. To what extent they managed to not act upon their desires is not known. The only testimony that remains are the ambiguous observations of Maintenon's friend Madame de Caylus who said that Madame de Maintenon was visibly upset before deciding to take communion at the Easter Mass of 1683.

Maintenon had only to wait a few months to dispel any qualms of conscience she might have had. Louis XIV's queen Marie-Thérèse died on July 30, 1683, and on October 9, she and Louis married, albeit secretly in a ceremony that denied her any royal inheritance and official queenly sta-tus—not having descended from royal blood, she would be a "morganatic" queen. The king's confessor, Père La Chaise, for whom the Paris cemetery is named, said the mass at Versailles.

After they began their conjugal life together, Madame de Maintenon wrote of the strain of being perpetually called upon by the king. He worked at a desk in her room, and interrupted her constantly to ask her opinion, causing her to complain that she could rarely even eat her supper in peace. He had come to rely on her counsel when burdened with worries both personal (the death of the Dauphin in 1711), and public (the bankruptcy of the country and famine throughout France in 1709). As a consequence, many of Maintenon's enemies at court resented her power and falsely impugned her for Louis's wrong-headed policies, such as his revocation of the 1596 Edict of Nantes which had given freedom to Protestants to practice their religion.

Madame de Maintenon's plodding, if calculated, rise from destitute origins to wife of the "Sun King" was anomalous and controversial. Though astrologer Barbé's prediction of 1666 did come to pass—a king would love her and she would reign—Maintenon shunned the dazzle of court and jealously guarded (as much as possible in the royal spotlight) her private life with Louis. She told her lady-in-waiting when she burned the king's letters after his death that no one would ever know what she meant to the monarch.

Sites

Hôtel de l'Impécuniosité
56, rue de Turenne (3rd arr.)
Métro: Chemin Vert
Paul Scarron's nickname for the *hôtel* where he and his wife hosted their soirées is typical of his wit. At the time the street name was rue Neuve Saint-Louis.

Hôtel d'Albret
31, rue des Francs Bourgeois (4th arr.)
Métro: St. Paul
Built by Anne de Montmorency in 1550, the owner of the *hôtel* in 1667 was César-Phoebus d'Albret, Comte de Miossens, described by his biographer as "a *maréchal de France* who fainted at the sight of a young wild boar." He hosted a succession of elite guests, among whom his cousin, the German Marquis de Montespan, was a favorite. In 1630 François Mansart was charged with additions to the building, and in 1744 the façade was completed by the architect Vautrain. Classified as an historical monument, the Hôtel d'Albret is the Center for cultural affairs for the city of Paris.

Site of Maintenon's house
Vicinity of 114, rue de Vaugirard (6th arr.)
Métro: Falguière or Saint Placide
The house where Louis XIV's children were lodged under the care of Françoise de Maintenon was located outside the city walls on rue Vaugirard, in the general area today of the Allée Maintenon.

Château de Fontainebleau
Fontainebleau
Tel: 01 60 71 50 70
www.musee-chateau-fontainebleau.fr
Daily except Tuesday 9:30am to 6pm;
October–March 9:30am to 5pm
Occupied by royalty since the twelfth century, the Palais de Fontainebleau became the vacation residence of Louis XIV in the 1660s. Madame de Maintenon's rooms there can be visited. In 1682 Louis moved his court to Versailles where he and Maintenon were secretly married.

St.-Cyr-l'Ecole
26 kilometers southwest of Paris
In 1686 Madame de Maintenon founded the St.-Cyr-l'Ecole, a school for girls from poor noble families like hers. Louis supported the effort wholeheart-

edly and sometimes performed (often missing his cue) in the plays Racine wrote for student performances there. Built by Mansart four kilometers west of Versailles, it was transformed into a military school by Napoleon in 1808, severely damaged in World War II, and rebuilt in 1964.

✳ *Le Roi danse*
(The King is Dancing)
Director: Gérard Corbiau
Cast: Benoît Magimel
K-Star, 2000
An elaborate costume drama of the rise of King Louis XIV to the peak of his power.

✳ *Saint-Cyr*
Director: Patricia Mazuy
Cast: Isabelle Huppert
Archipel 35, 2000
The film focuses on Madame de Maintenon's controversial influence on the girls at the school she had built near Versailles.

GABRIELLE·EMILIE·DE·BRETEVIL·MARQUISE·DV·CHASTELET·LORRAINE·

Gabrielle Emilie Le Tonnelier de Breteuil, Madame du Châtelet

(1706–1749)

PHILOSOPHER-PHYSICIST WHOSE
CALCULATION OF THE FORCE OF
MOVING BODIES WAS A LINK IN THE
CHAIN LEADING TO EINSTEIN'S
THEORY OF RELATIVITY

In 1735 Voltaire complained to his friend Ciderville:

Poetry is no longer in fashion in Paris. Everyone is becoming a geometrician and physicist. Everyone dabbles in "reason." Sentiment, imagination and the graces are banished . . . and belles-lettres have dropped out of sight. . . . It is not that I am angry that philosophy be cultivated, but I wouldn't want it to become a tyrant. . . . I want to go from an experiment to an opera.[1]

It was no wonder that Emilie du Châtelet and Voltaire's love affair and, later, friendship endured for more than two decades; both were engaged in everything on his list. Together they conducted experiments in their lab for essays they wrote "On the nature of fire." At other times *Madame*, as Voltaire called her, was either shut up with geometry and algebra tutors in the Faubourg Saint-Honoré or singing a full opera for friends in the evening. Voltaire kept belles-lettres very much alive, writing plays for the Comédie-Française or satire, which sometimes landed him in the Bastille. In the meantime Emilie du Châtelet was hailed for translations of works by the German philosopher Leibniz—one Paris admirer said that "Everybody understands monads [single organisms] since the Leibnizians made the brilliant acquisition of Mme du Châtelet."[2] And though her talents lay in science, it was her passion for theater that bordered on tyranny. As an exhausted guest wrote from Châtelet's country estate:

We can't breathe here. . . . We perform The Prodigal Son and one other play in three acts, for which we must rehearse. We have rehearsed Zaire till three in the morning; tomorrow we perform Serenade. We must curl our hair, put our shoes on, be properly dressed, listen to opera; it's hell. . . . We counted last night that in twenty-four hours, we rehearsed and performed thirty-three acts, tragedies, operas, and comedies alike.[3]

Since childhood Emilie de Breteuil had pursued all kinds of knowledge.

Maurice Quentin de la Tour: Madame du Châtelet
Private Collection / The Bridgeman Art Library International

Her parents had her tutored in math, science, Latin, Italian, and English. At ten she listened to intellectuals like scientist Fontenelle and the young Voltaire in the family's salon in their *hôtel* near the Tuileries. Eager to show off his young math genius during these sessions, her father would have her divide nine digits in her head to impress his guests.

To assure her a noble lineage he arranged for her marriage to the Marquis du Châtelet, a man who soon realized that he was no match for his brilliant wife. After the births of their three children, the Marquise du Châtelet and her husband, who traveled often on military maneuvers, saw each other only on occasion. Noble marriages like theirs were primarily business affairs concerned with combining estates and properties. Though the Marquis was always pleased to be reunited with his wife, in time he came to accept Voltaire as her more suitable companion.

Voltaire was reintroduced to Emilie, become Madame du Châtelet, in 1733, when friends brought her along to his bachelor apartment in the rundown Marais neighborhood. He had just returned from London and was reading Newton and Locke, of little interest to Parisian philosophers who remained loyal to Descartes. Emilie, he discovered, had a scientific mind and wanted to study Newton and Locke too.

Before long Châtelet and Voltaire became what he called "the most voluptuous philosophers," shuttling regularly between Paris society and work in pastoral solitude. Monsieur de Villefort, a visitor to their château in Cirey, called them Venus and Adonis and described their daily routine. In the evening after work each emerged from their room:

Presently a bell rang and they all went to the dining-room which had two hatches, one for the food and the other for the dirty plates. No servant appeared; they helped themselves. The food and wine were exquisite and the supper very long. When it was over, another bell rang to announce moral and philosophical readings. The guest was asked his permission and the readings took place. An hour later a bell rang for bedtime; the party broke up. At four in the morning there was another bell. A servant came to ask M. de Villefort if he would care to join a poetry reading which he did out of curiosity. Next day they had a picnic. Venus and Adonis in a chariot, the Stranger [Villefort] on horseback, proceeded to a little wood where they ate cutlets. They were followed by a second carriage full of books. The husband never appeared.[4]

In Paris, the couple frequented the *haut-monde.* When they bought the palatial Hôtel Lambert on the Ile Saint-Louis, they worried no one would come visit them in their new city residence. Few friends did since the *île* had become less fashionable with limited access from the Right Bank. Later, however, in lodgings in the busy neighborhood of rue du Faubourg Saint-Honoré, their salons consistently drew large numbers.

For Châtelet, town connections were vital to her research and continued education. There she studied with mathematicians and scientists who could help round out those areas where her knowledge was deficient. Even though formal training was unavailable to women at the University, her noble status made it possible to engage tutors, some of whom were respected authorities of the day: Maupertuis, Koenig, and Clairaut. They served as mentors and then colleagues as she formulated her own theory in physics.

Before long the results of her experiments stirred up a debate among academicians in Paris. In 1740 she published her *Institutions of Physics* which presented her calculation of the force of moving bodies. In the book she corrected an error in physicist Dortous de Mairan's treatise on the subject. His calculations were based on Cartesian dead force (mv: mass times velocity); hers relied on Leibniz's dynamics (mv^2: mass times acceleration). She wrote, "According to him, the velocity of a moving body remains constant and does not accelerate" (which was inaccurate; Châtelet's correct calculation would be an important link in the chain leading to Einstein's theory of relativity). She concludes: "Thus, the more seductive the arguments [Mairan's], the more I feel obliged to make you see that they do not apply to the doctrine of force."[5] Mairan, the newly elected Secretary-in-Perpetuity of the Académie des Sciences, was mortified to be found wanting by a woman. He accused her of not reading the work carefully and not understanding it, mistakes that, he said, were due to her delicate female condition, "the source of her illusions." Châtelet was quick

French School (18th century): Portrait of the Young Voltaire

Musée Antoine Lecuyer, Saint-Quentin, France / Giraudon / The Bridgeman Art Library International

to challenge his slur, "As for what you call 'the most delicate sources of illusion,' when I know what you mean by it, I will try to respond." In the thick of her argument with Mairan, Emilie du Châtelet wrote to her friend, d'Argental, "I'm not Secretary of the Academy, but I am right and that is worth all the titles . . . ."[6]

A secondary gain from the high-profile dispute, which the scientific community followed in its open letters, was the opportunity it gave her to refute an earlier charge by her teacher Koenig that in *Institutions* she had claimed credit for his ideas. Both Maupertuis and Bernoulli, colleagues with whom she corresponded during her work, knew the charges to be false, though Maupertuis did not immediately come to her public defense. The argument with Mairan would eventually prove to her scientist readers that she alone, and not Koenig, was the author of the ideas in her book.

But *Institutions of Physics* was not just for physicists. The 450-page tome integrated Newtonian physics and the philosophy of Leibniz to make complicated science accessible to French readers in a clear, thorough translation and commentary. Voltaire stayed out of the debate with Marian, unlike Paris society women, who took up the pen in support of Châtelet's position.

Finally in 1741 academician Maupertuis broke ranks and praised the Marquise's work, confirming her results. With that battle behind her, in 1745 Châtelet embarked on her next project, a translation of Newton's Latin treatise on physics, the *Principia*.

At the time she and Voltaire were renting separate floors at 43, rue Traversière (today rue Molière). They had lived together as if they were a married couple for more than ten years, reading and commenting on one another's work, even when their romantic desires found satisfaction elsewhere: Voltaire was involved with a Madame Denis and Châtelet fell in love with the poet Jean-François de Saint-Lambert.

As a result of her affair Châtelet found herself pregnant, a condition she knew had serious risks at forty-three. As her dreaded due date approached, she arranged for Voltaire, the Marquis du Châtelet, and Saint-Lambert to be with her for the birth. Her friend Stanislas II, King of Poland, provided her with rooms in his château at Lunéville in Lorraine for the sake of privacy during the delivery.

Believing she would die in childbirth, she worked at a feverish pace to finish her translation and commentary on Newton. When the contractions started, she was at her desk and had not prepared for the delivery. The infant was born so quickly that Châtelet's maid (as Voltaire told the story) had to place the newborn on a geometry book. After the danger of childbirth had passed, the men joked in her recovery room where she continued to work in bed. A few days later she came down with a fever, but when she appeared to improve and was resting comfortably, her companions left her bedside. During their brief absence she slipped from consciousness and died.

Voltaire was inconsolable and blamed Saint-Lambert for having "killed" her. In despair he delayed his return to Paris, unable to face acquaintances who were all talking about Châtelet's death. Closeted in his room, he wrote to his friend, "It is not a mistress I have lost but half of myself, a soul for which my soul seems to have been made."[7]

Hôtel Lambert today
Author photo

When the time came for his public eulogy, he painted a multifaceted portrait of his long-time companion. Regarding her style he said:

Her writing is closer to that of Pascal and Nicole [d'Oresme, a fourteenth-century scientist] than to that of Mme de Sévigné. Yet the firm discipline and the vigorous character of her mind did not render her inaccessible to the beauty of sentiment. She was affected by the charm of poetry and of eloquence and no ear was ever more sensitive to harmony. She knew the best poetry by heart and could not suffer mediocre verse.

Speaking of *Institutions* as a "masterpiece of reason and eloquence," he applauded her for "bringing to readers a method and clarity which Leibniz never possessed." Voltaire, being a man of his time, could only praise Châtelet's accomplishments as compared to those of men. Of her *Principia* he said, "The more astonishing is that a woman should have been capable of an enterprise that required such penetration and so persistent a labor . . ."[8]

Maupertuis's earlier speech summed up Châtelet's achievement in a field dominated by men:

At the beginning of the year a work [Institutions] appeared which would honor our country, if it had been by one of the principal members of the Academies of Europe. This work is however by a woman and, what is even more of a marvel is that this woman having been raised in the dissipations attached to high birth, had no other master than her genius and her application to instruct her.[9]

Sites

Hôtel Lambert
2, rue Saint-Louis-en-l'Ile (4th arr.)
Métro: Pont-Marie
Madame du Châtelet and Voltaire bought the Hôtel Lambert in 1739 but spent little time there. It was too remote from society on the Right Bank.

Now a private residence closed to the public, the *hôtel* was built by Le Vau with sculptures by Le Sueur and Le Brun during the mid-seventeenth century when the Ile-Notre-Dame was renamed for Saint Louis and transformed into a stylish quarter. Extending from its entrance at rue Saint-Louis-en-l'Ile across to the Quai d'Anjou, almost to the tip of the island, it had lush gardens adorned with curved portals, ionic pilasters, sculpted lions, grotesque masques, and palms — conventional emblems of the riches of its occupants.

Académie des Sciences (Institut de France)
23, Quai de Conti (6th arr.)
Métro: Pont Neuf or St.-Michel
www.academie-sciences.fr
Officially instated in 1699 by Louis XIV, the Académie des Sciences is a branch

of the Institut de France which encompasses four other academies: Beaux-Arts, Belles-Lettres, Académie Française, and Académie des sciences morales et politiques.

Institut Emilie du Châtelet Musée de l'Homme (Chaillot Museum of Natural History)

17, Place du Trocadéro (16th arr.)
Métro: Trocadéro
www.emilieduchatelet.org
In 2006 the institute, housed at the Chaillot Museum of Natural History in the Musée de l'Homme, was established for research on women, sex, and gender. It offers ongoing conferences, listed on their website.

✳ **"Einstein's Big Idea"**
    (*NOVA* **PBS broadcast)**
    Director: Gary Johnstone
    Cast: John Lithgow, Shirley Hender-
    son, Aidan McArdle
    Darlow Smithson Productions, 2005
    One of the vignettes about Einstein's predecessors is devoted to Emilie du Châtelet for her calculation of the force of moving bodies.

✳ *Divine Émilie*
    Director: Arnaud Sélignac
    Cast: Léa Drucker, Thierry Fremont,
    Aurore Clément
    BFC Productions, 2007
    In French. Aired on France 3 television, *Divine Émilie* has not yet been released in the United States.

Marie-Jeanne (Manon) Phlipon, Madame Roland

(1754–1793)
GIRONDIN ACTIVIST DURING THE
FRENCH REVOLUTION AND HEROIC
VICTIM OF THE REIGN OF TERROR

"It was the worst of times" when Manon Roland looked for the last time at her childhood home on the Quai de l'Horloge from the tumbril on the way to her execution.

The agonizing ride lasted about an hour. Leaving the Conciergerie prison on the Ile de la Cité on November 8, 1793, the cart rattled across the Pont au Change up the Quai de la Mégisserie. As it passed the corner of the Pont Neuf, she noticed her friend, Sophie Grandchamp, who later recalled seeing Manon Roland talking to a fellow condemned prisoner who was next to her in the wagon. Roland, herself composed and cheerful, was attempting to comfort and encourage him. At the bridge the wagon turned onto rue de la Monnaie, then left onto rue Saint-Honoré. It rolled past the open doors of the Church of St. Roch, whose altars and walls had been stripped, and the building next door which served as the headquarters of the Jacobin club whose members had sentenced Roland

Madame Roland being led to the revolutionary tribunal

Archives, Musée de la Ville de Paris / Musée Carnavalet, Paris, France

to death. "Citizens" along the street wearing the tricolor cockade stared or heckled the pair as the rickety carriage wobbled by. In the Place de la Révolution (now Place de la Concorde) it came to a halt where the guillotine loomed over the blood-stained pavement.

Manon Roland and her husband Jean-Marie had the misfortune of being Girondins when the Jacobins came to power in 1793. Jacobin and Girondin factions vehemently disagreed on how to bring down the monarchy. Jacobins wanted central control of power in Paris; moderate Girondins called for a vote in the provinces.

Much had happened since the "best of times" in 1789 when the Bastille fell and the women from the Faubourg Saint-Antoine marched to Versailles to bring King Louis XVI back to Paris. The French Republic was declared in late September 1792; Louis XVI and Marie Antoinette were beheaded in January and October 1793. The property

of the nobility had been sold; churches had been plundered and transformed from places of worship into secular meeting places called Temples to Reason; the Church of St. Geneviève had been renamed the Panthéon; the Sainte-Chapelle on the Ile de la Cité had become a flour warehouse; and revolutionaries, taking the statues of the Old Testament kings on the façade of Notre Dame for the kings of France, had "decapitated" them (some are in the Cluny Museum).

The man responsible for Manon Roland's arrest, the Jacobin Robespierre, had been a regular at the Rolands' political salon in their modest *hôtel* on rue de la Harpe (near the corner of boulevard Saint-Germain in the 5th arrondissement), where guests included Thomas Paine, author of "Declaration of the Rights of Man;" Danton, a compatriot who would later turn against them during the Terror; the mayor of Paris; and others.

These meetings at the Rolands' salon, where leaders discussed the direction of the Revolution, were for Manon Roland the dramatic climax of her life. Her marriage to Roland, twenty years her senior and a man of mediocre abilities, had been a disappointment, as was her unremarkable daughter Eudora.

As an intellectually endowed child and young adult, Manon Phlipon thought she was destined to play a far greater part in history. Having enjoyed comforts slightly above her bourgeois rank, she was given a more thorough education than others of her class. By nine she had cut her moral teeth on Plutarch, Augustine, St. Francis de Sales, and the preacher Bossuet. At fourteen she devoured the correspondence of Madame de Sévigné along with the works of Voltaire, Pascal, Descartes, Locke, and Montesquieu. In her memoirs Manon Roland reflected on how these influences prepared her for her role as a revolutionary, recalling her despair as a girl of twelve, that she had not been a citizen of Sparta or Rome. Yet in the Revolution, she discerned the ideals upon which she had been nurtured. She believed that liberty was a result of two things: morality, which is responsible for a just legal system, and enlightenment, which affirms the rights of men and women. The

The women's march to Versailles on October 5th, 1789
Archives, Musée de la Ville de Paris / Musée Carnavalet, Paris, France

Revolution, she believed, would bring to an end to the shame of inequality and would be a force to guarantee the advancement of humanity.

That "now" had arrived and after her first tastes of "liberty," she drafted passionate articles in the Girondin press and eloquent speeches in praise of the revolution. On June 8, 1792, in her husband's name—he was Interior Minister—she wrote a letter to the king chiding him for opposing the establishment of a National Guard to protect Paris:

This is not time to retreat or to temporize. The revolution has been made in people's minds; it will be accomplished and cemented at the cost of bloodshed unless wisdom forestalls evils which it is still possible to avoid. . . .[1]

Louis dismissed Jean-Marie Roland immediately, a consequence his wife nonetheless savored as a moral triumph. In December, summoned before the Convention (the new name for the National Assembly) to answer questions about the Rolands' alleged complicity with royalists, Manon Roland so impressed its members that the session ended with a standing ovation for her. She said:

Motherland is not just a word which the imagination takes pleasure in embellishing. It is a being to whom one makes sacrifices, to whom one grows more attached every day through the cares it imposes, who has been created by great efforts, who grows in the midst of anxiety, and who is loved as much for what it costs as for what it promises.[2]

But by the following spring the Rolands' Girondin friends were accused of conspiracy against the Republic. On May 31st, Jacobin authorities knocked on the Rolands' door to arrest Jean-Marie. Irate, Manon Roland rushed to the Marsan Pavilion in the Tuileries Palace where the Convention was attempting to hold its session. In the tumult crowds pushed through the entrance while those in the galleries interrupted deputies at the podium. A preeminent Girondin saw Manon elbow her way toward him and shouted above the din that the tide had changed: members would not allow her to speak. Undaunted, she told him that she was fearless and that if she were allowed to take the floor, she was prepared to speak the truth that she felt should be heard throughout the Republic. She knew her refusal to stay silent might set a courageous example and cautioned

the Girondin to warn his comrades. When she returned home, authorities were waiting, and they promptly arrested her. Her husband had escaped, but she had refused to leave Paris. She explained in her memoir that if the Rolands' enemies wanted to go through the staged motions of questioning her at a mock trial, she was confident she would have no trouble confounding them. . . . And if they again resorted to actions like like the September massacres, she would be willing to give her life rather than stand by and watch the destruction of her ideals; indeed, she felt it would be an honor to be among those patriots unjustly sent to their deaths. Counted among them she was. Incarcerated in the Abbaye, then Pélagie prisons, she decided on October 3rd to starve herself to death, but changed her mind eleven days later in the hopes of testifying on behalf of Girondins at their trial on October 24th. Her plan was to speak in their defense, then to take poison in full view of the court, an heroic gesture which would have allowed

her to preempt her execution. Denied the poison promised by a friend and then the opportunity to appear by the court, she was transferred to the Conciergerie, the last stop before her execution.

Defiant and proud to the end, she uttered her final words on the scaffold, "O Liberty, what crimes are committed in thy name."

Sites

Childhood home of Marie-Jeanne Phlipon Roland

41, Quai de l'Horloge (1st arr.)
Métro: Pont Neuf

Manon Phlipon lived above her father's shop in the Place Dauphine where the master engraver and his apprentices made picture frames, snuff boxes, watch cases, and a variety of jeweled luxury items. A plaque marking the site reads: "Madame Roland, born in Paris on March 17, 1754, died November 8, 1793, was raised in this house."

When the Pont Neuf was completed in 1605, red brick houses were built in perfect symmetry to form the Place Dauphine, named for the *dauphin* Louis XIII, the son of Henri IV, who oversaw the construction of the bridge. The "prow" of the island to the west, the Square du Vert Galant (Henri IV's nickname, the womanizer), accessed by the stairs that descend from the bridge to the river, is at the level of the Ile de la Cité and other islands in the Seine during Roman times.

Conciergerie

2, boulevard du Palais (1st arr.)
Tel. 01 53 40 60 80
Métro: Cité or St. Michel
Daily 9:30am to 6pm, November–February 9am to 5pm

The Conciergerie, formerly the Royal Palace, was transformed into a prison during the Revolution. The cells, including that of Marie Antoinette, can be visited on guided tours.

Place de la Bastille

(4th arr.)
Métro: Bastille

On July 14, 1789, crowds supported by National Guards stormed the Bastille prison for arms and ammunition stored there. The seven inmates were released and the fortress dismantled. In its place is the July column (honoring the July Monarchy of 1830), topped with a statue of the Spirit of Liberty. On the street an outline of the Bastille marks its location. Some stones remain at the Square Henri Galli, near the Métro Sully-Morland in the 4th arrondissement.

Hôtel de Ville

Place de l'Hotel de Ville (4th arr.)
Métro: Hôtel de Ville

This large *place* marks the point of departure of the Women's March on October 5, 1789, during which a crowd of women from the Faubourg Saint-Antoine filled the square, broke into Hôtel de Ville (City Hall) offices, and destroyed municipal records. Armed with pikes and swords, they set out for Versailles to air their grievances to King Louis XVI. The march lasted two days and ended with the king's return to Paris where he could be watched more closely during the unfolding events. As historian Jules Michelet wrote: "Men captured the Bastille, but it was women who captured the king."

Site of the Tuileries Palace

(1st arr.)
Jardin des Tuileries
Métro: Tuileries

The Tuileries Palace, which no longer stands, connected the two western pavilions of the Louvre at the entrance of the gardens. The National Assembly was located on the Terrasse des Feuillants along rue de Rivoli. Two months after the royal family fled from the palace, they were shut up in the Temple prison in the Square du Temple and the Convention, now the new name for the National Assembly, moved to the (north) Marsan Pavilion of the Tuileries Palace.

One woman insurgent who pursued aristocrats at the Tuileries was revolutionary Anne-Josephe Terwagne. She wore a riding-habit with a saber at her waist, and donned a plumed hat. She campaigned for a woman's right to join the military and drilled her squadron of women at the Champ de Mars.

Convent des Carmes

70, rue de Vaugirard (6th arr.)
Métro: Rennes
On Sat. at 3pm there is a free guided tour of the church and grounds (in French but the guide may be able to translate) focusing on the events of the September massacre there in 1792.
The Church of St. Joseph des Carmes is open for services Sat. and Thurs. at 6:15pm, Sun. 11am, Fri. 12:15, Wed. 12:45pm

On September 2, 1792, mobs slaughtered 116 priests and lay prisoners at the convent, which had been transformed into a prison. The cloister and chapel are open for visits during the day. The remains of victims are buried in the crypt.

The Abbaye Prison was located at Place Jacques Copeau opposite the Church of Saint-Germain-des-Prés, on the boulevard Saint-Germain. It was one of the many prisons where clergy and loyalists were thrown onto the mercy of the crowds during the September 1792 massacres. Though the executions appeared to be spontaneous acts of mob violence, they had been carefully planned in advance by revolutionaries.

❋ *Danton*

> **Director: Andrzej Wajda**
> **Cast: Gérard Depardieu**
> **Gaumont International, 1983**
> Profile of one leader who came to power during the Revolution, only to be guillotined later.

❋ *La Nuit de Varennes*

> **Director: Ettore Scola**
> **Cast: Marcello Mastroianni, Harvey Keitel, Jean-Louis Barrault**
> **Gaumont, 1982**
> The film focuses on the royal family's attempted escape from Paris shortly after the revolution began.

Elisabeth Vigée Le Brun

(1755–1842)
PORTRAITIST OF MARIE ANTOINETTE
AND EUROPEAN COURT FIGURES

Every day visitors to the Palace of Versailles walk past Elisabeth Vigée Le Brun's painting of Marie Antoinette and her children. Commissioned during the reign of Louis XVI to counter charges of bad mothering by French subjects who resented his Austrian queen, it originally hung in the Hall of Mirrors. When her son, the Dauphin, died, the grieving queen had it moved out of sight, a decision that saved the portrait from destruction when angry mobs gained entry to parts of the palace on October 5, 1789.

During those riotous days, Elisabeth Vigée Le Brun was nowhere near Versailles. As the royal family was being escorted under guard back to Paris, she was home at rue Cléry preparing to flee. Closeness to the queen could be grounds for arrest. Disguised as a laborer, she boarded a carriage with her five-year-old daughter, Julie. Her husband, her brother, and her painter friend Hubert Robert accompanied them as far as the barrier at the city limits, after which mother and daughter continued the journey on their own. By midnight their *diligence* had crossed

through the revolutionary faubourg Saint-Antoine quarter.

The ride was both depressing and alarming. Macabre accounts of aristocrats' murders and gleeful predictions of the inevitable fate of "the baker and the baker's wife" (the derogatory epithet for Louis XVI and Marie Antoinette) swirled about them. To Elisabeth's added consternation, one passenger, who earlier had gloated over the impending demise of the king and queen, began discussing a recent Salon exhibit where Vigée Le Brun's self-portrait with Julie had been displayed. Terrified, she pulled her shawl closer to her face.

For weeks Vigée Le Brun had been living in fear. As Marie Antoinette's official portraitist, she had reason to worry. Revolutionary *sansculotte* women waved their fists at her in the street, and frightened loyalist friends told of ragtag mobs who menaced them in their carriages and chanted: "Next year, you'll be [running] behind the carriages and *we'll* be riding."[1] Among those arrested and imprisoned was her friend Hubert Robert; taken for an aristocrat, he

Elisabeth Vigée Le Brun: Self Portrait, 1790
Galleria degli Uffizi, Florence, Italy / The Bridgeman Art Library International

escaped the guillotine by pure luck when another prisoner with the same name was mistakenly hauled off to the scaffold. She recalled concerts only a year before in the salon of her Hôtel de Lubert, when guests' most serious concerns were debates over favorite composers Puccini and Gluck.

Vigée Le Brun was well known in Paris. At fifteen, the young painter already had a steady stream of noble patrons walking through her door on rue Coquillère near Les Halles: "[A]lready my young reputation attracted visits of a great number of foreigners. Several highly placed Russians came to see me, among them the famous Count Orloff, one of the assassins of Peter III [of Russia]. . . ."[2] In 1779 she was appointed at Court, and three years later the painter Joseph Vernet proposed her candidacy for membership in the Royal Academy of Painting and Sculpture.

Since its founding in 1648 during the regency of Anne d'Autriche, the Academy had dictated artistic taste through the work of its members, which was exhibited in the Salon d'Apollon in the Louvre. When Vigée Le Brun was proposed as a candidate, Academy president M. Pierre refused to consider her, claiming it already had enough women. Besides, the Academy declared that women "by their nature" did not contribute to the progress of the arts and hence were not permitted to take the oath of allegiance to the institution. In 1702, members had established a quota of four women, with no obligation to fill *all four* seats. (Out of 450 artists who had become members since the Academy's inception, only fifteen had been women.)

In her memoirs Vigée le Brun explained how Pierre was overruled by a coalition of her supporters:

His opposition could have been fatal for me, if at this time all the true amateurs had not also been associated with the Academy of painting, and if they had not formed, in my favor, a cabal against that of M. Pierre.[3]

Though she states further on that Pierre started the rumor that she was admitted by order of the king and not by merit, she implies otherwise, "Indeed the king and queen were in favor of my admission to the Academy; but no more than that."

After being pressured to admit Vigée Le Brun, Pierre was outraged by her "reception piece" (the painting submitted for her induction into the Academy), painted in a genre deemed inappropriate for a woman. Protocol required members to assign the candidate a specific genre. The most prestigious was the "history painting," closed to women. For them, the lower ranks of "portrait" or "still life" were reserved. Vigée Le Brun, confident of reception, preempted their dictates and presented a history painting that caused no end of controversy. An admirer of her work remarked:

I do not know in which rank the Academy placed Madame Le Brun, whether it was history, or genre [still life], or the portrait, but she is not unworthy of any, even the first. I consider her reception piece as very likely to allow her admission in the first rank. It is "Peace Bringing Back Abundance," an allegory as natural as ingenious: one could not have chosen better for the situation.[4]

In apparent retaliation for Vigée Le Brun's coup, further restrictions in the arts were imposed on women, who were already shut out of the Paris Ecole Royale des Elèves Protégés. "In order to preserve women's virtue," the Minister of the Arts decreed, female art students were no longer allowed to secure lodgings in the Louvre, as was the custom, or to study in group classes there.

The new limitations did not apply to Vigée Le Brun, already an accomplished artist with a following in Paris and abroad. During her twelve years in exile with her daughter, she garnered patrons at royal and imperial courts throughout Europe and Russia.

No sooner did she settle in a court or city than some official would request a portrait. In Naples both Count Scawronski and Sir William Hamilton vied to be the first to have theirs done. In Moscow, within ten to twelve days of her arrival she had started six portraits. In St. Petersburg the dust was hardly off her shoes when, she writes:

The next day Count Stroganoff came to me on behalf of the emperor, who commissioned me to do his portrait in half length and on horseback. Hardly had the news spread, when a crowd of courtiers flocked to my quarters to request copies either on horseback or half length, little did it matter, provided that they had a portrait of Alexander.[5]

Elisabeth Vigée Le Brun: Marie-Antoinette and her Children, 1787

Noble women clamored for her to paint them in her less formal, original style. She said:

Since I detested the outfits women wore then, I tried to make them look more picturesque, . . . to drape them as I wished. Shawls were no longer worn; but I used wide scarves, lightly wreathed around the body and on the arms, trying to imitate the draperies of Raphael and Dominiquin. . . . Besides I did not like powdered hair. . . .[6]

Even Pope Pius VI in Rome requested a portrait, his only stipulation being that she remain veiled during his sittings. (She refused the commission.)

When she returned to Paris in 1802 when the bloody revolution was over, one of her first commissions was from Napoleon. Vigée Le Brun later wrote:

. . . He sent me M. Denon to commission on his behalf a portrait of his sister, Madame Murat. I did not believe it possible to refuse, even though I was only paid eighteen hundred francs for this portrait, that is less than half of what I usually received for portraits of this size.[7]

In her memoirs, Vigée Le Brun recalls that the day after she returned to Paris she went to Versailles to see her painting of Marie Antoinette and her children. Napoleon had ordered it to be taken away because crowds came constantly to view what was anathema during the early years of the Republic: an endearing portrait of a former queen. The custodian of the painting did not carry out the order, but left it in a corner turned against the wall. When he recognized "Madame Le Brun" and eagerly showed her the painting, she tried to give him something for his trouble. But, she wrote, "he obstinately refused, saying that because of me he was already earning enough money."[8] The stream of visitors — the curious, or those who still regretted the demise of the monarchy — paid him well for the chance to see her painting of the queen and her royal children.

The revolution had not entirely expunged the past or everyone's ambivalence toward it. On July 8, 1814, the monarchy was reinstated with Louis XVIII's return to Paris in the midst of joyful refrains. Soon afterwards, Elisabeth Vigée Le Brun saw her painting of Marie Antoinette and her children exhibited at the royal Salon d'Apollon in the Louvre.

Sites

Home of Vigée Le Brun
Hôtel de Lubert
16, rue de Cléry (2nd arr.)
Métro: Sentier
In this *hôtel* Vigée Le Brun hosted salons for her friends who for the most part were aristocrats but also included artists like Hubert Robert and associates of her husband, who was an art dealer.

Musée du Louvre
(1st arr.)
Tel: 01 40 20 50 50
Métro: Louvre-Rivoli
Daily except Tuesday 9am to 6pm;
Wednesday, Friday until 10pm
www.louvre.fr
In the Louvre, Vigée Le Brun's controversial reception piece, *Peace Bringing Back Abundance*, and one self-portrait are in the Sully wing, in the Salle Vigée Le Brun, room 52 of the French Painting section. Her portrait of Hubert Robert is in the Sully wing, second floor, Salle Fragonard, room 48. Her self-portrait of 1789, exhibited just before she fled Paris, is in the Denon wing, first floor, Salle Daru, room 75.

Jacques-Louis David was so struck by her portrait of the composer Paesiello, exhibited in the Louvre as a pendant to his, that he told his students: "One would think my canvas was painted by a woman and the portrait of Paesiello was painted by a man."

Musée Jacquemart André
158, boulevard Haussmann (8th arr.)
Tel: 01 45 62 11 59
Métro: Miromesnil or St.-Philippe-du-Roule
Daily 10am to 6pm
www.musee-jacquemart-andre.com/en/jacquemart
Near the Champs Elysées, this mansion houses several paintings by Vigée Le Brun. The nineteenth-century *hôtel particulier* is an architectural gem with art from various periods. (Other Paris museums with her paintings: Cognac Jay at 8, rue Elzévir in the 3rd arrondissement and the Camondo at 63, rue de Monceau in the 8th arrondissement.)

Château de Versailles
RER C: Versailles-Rive Gauche-Château de Versailles
www.chateauversailles.fr
Daily except Monday 9am to 6:30pm, November 1–March 31 9am to 5:30pm
Vigée Le Brun's painting of Marie Antoinette and her children is in the Grand Couvert Room (the Guard Room for the Queen).

✳ *Marie Antoinette*
   Director: Sofia Coppola
   Cast: Kirsten Dunst, Jason Schwartzman, Judy Davis, Rip Torn
   Columbia Pictures Corporation, 2006
   The movie gives a feel for the opulence and waste of Louis XVI's court. For a furtive moment one catches a glimpse of Vigée Le Brun painting the queen and her children.

Eliza Rachel Félix

(1821–1858)
ACTRESS WHOSE INNOVATIVE STYLE
REVIVED THE MORIBUND COMÉDIE-
FRANÇAISE AND WHO BECAME A
SENSATION ON THE PARIS STAGE

When theater-goers returned to Paris in the fall of 1838, they found the moribund Théâtre Français, the national theater whose performances were held in the Comédie-Française on rue de Richelieu, risen from its ashes. During the summer months the young tragedienne Rachel had breathed new life into a classical repertoire—tragedies such as Racine's *Andromaque* and *Iphigénie*, and the works of seventeenth-century Molière and Corneille, whose collective legacy was synonymous with the glories of France. At the time Rachel began to appear on its stage, the Théâtre Français had lost all appeal and was competing for audiences with popular theaters' comedies, melodramas, and thrillers.

While the Paris elite had been trickling in to the Comédie-Française, the masses packed the lowbrow *théâtres du boulevard*. At the national theater, actors delivered the lines of Roman and Greek heroes with restrained emotions, in an inflected, declamatory style. Popular theaters featured passionate protagonists, born of the nineteenth-century Romantic movement, in action-packed plays where violence appeared on stage, instead of being decorously recounted by witnesses as the old conventions of drama required. In her revival of the traditional repertory, Rachel infused the cold, classical figures with a fire that intensified their tragic pathos. An American actor visiting Paris reported that in "that little bag of bones with the marble face and flaming eyes," he saw "demoniacal power."[1]

But it had been Rachel's contralto voice that caught the attention of the music teacher Choron, who heard her one day on the street singing for money. The Félixes were poor Jewish peddlers who had emigrated from Switzerland to Paris and settled in a flat behind the Hôtel de Ville. Choron brought the ten-year-old urchin to the Conservatoire where his actor friend Saint-Aulaire tutored Rachel in its chant-like diction and stock gestures.

When Rachel made her unremarkable debut in 1835 (at the Théâtre du Gymnase on the Left Bank), it was clear that the Théâtre Française was heading for insolvency. Premonitions of

Friederike Emile August O'Connell: Rachel

decline had been felt five years earlier when Victor Hugo challenged the conservative establishment there with his Romantic play *Hernani*. That night rightist *anciens* and leftist *modernes* took to their battle stations. The elite first balcony sneered, booed, and drowned out the actors; the provocateur second tier retaliated with deafening applause and a confetti of greasy papers from sausage sandwiches. Balzac received a cabbage in his face while his friend Théophile Gautier berated the enemy:

. . . all these larvae of the past and of routine, all these enemies of art, the ideal, liberty and poetry, who wanted with their debilitated, trembling hands to keep the door closed to the future; and we felt in our hearts, the wild desire to scalp them with our tomahawk to decorate our belts; but in this battle, we would have run the risk of collecting fewer crops of hair than wigs. . . .[2]

The hostile spectacle made the eighteen-year-old Rachel's renewal of the classical plays all the more remarkable.

Without expressly intending to do so, she fused warring tastes. According to Flaubert, her acting style made the classical theater relevant to popular audiences — "She makes Corneille and Racine into contemporary geniuses, full of immediacy"[3] — while Victor Hugo's friend noted that baronesses and dukes who scorned the "vulgar" display of emotion in popular drama got their fill of it in the guise of Rachel's highbrow performances: "Society people go to see tragedies now as women of easy virtue go to Mass."[4]

Poet Alfred de Musset told of visiting her one evening in 1839 in her family's Marais apartment where she and her mother dined on a simple soup and vegetables. In the midst of the homely, domestic scene Rachel sat reading Racine's play *Phèdre* aloud, enthralled in the rhythms and beauty of its lines. Her ambition, she told him, was to play the great heroine.

She had already won rave reviews for playing Camille in Corneille's tragedy *Horace* where she exuded masculine strength with a disturbing, frisson-producing delivery. Pale, slight of build, with a deep, rasping voice and fiery eyes, she was more androgynous than beautiful, more powerful than charming.

A critic wrote of her performance:

One might simply mention the plainest, positively savage pleasure of Rachel, when she disgraces Horace's laurels, tramples all his beliefs under foot, mocks what he holds holy. She no longer cares about her words, her predicament, herself. Her face is distorted, her mouth agape as if from a bloody flux, her very tongue, it seems, parched, and her voice sometimes alters, breaks and turns into a strident shriek — a startling effect which completes the ghastly picture of frenzy and self-oblivion which you see before you.[5]

At the end of the play the Comte de Mole of the Académie Française, who believed she would restore the reputation of the Théâtre Français, expressed his gratitude hyperbolically: "Madame, you have saved the French language from destruction." "Sir," she replied, "my credit is the greater in view of the fact that I have never learned it."[6] Indeed, having arrived in Paris at nine years of age a Jewish girl from a family with no means, she had had no formal education, an irony for an actress who was quickly becoming the symbol of high culture and national pride.

Audiences heralded her as such in the eminent protagonists she played. They came to see her as a real life incarnation of the roles she played: Camille, the Roman "chaste virgin" challenger of the state; the biblical Judith, defender of the Jewish people; Jeanne d'Arc herself.

But when gossip spread of her numerous liaisons—the poet Musset, Count Alexandre Walewski (Napoleon Bonaparte's son), and the man who would become Napoleon III (Bonaparte's nephew)—she seemed more like Racine's decadent Phèdre, a role she finally played in 1843, whose sexual desire for her stepson Hippolyte turns criminal and destructive. George Henry Lewes wrote of her as consumed with erotic longing: "You felt that she was wasting away under the fire within, that she was standing on the verge of the grave with pallid face, hot eyes, emaciate frame—an awful ghastly apparition."[7]

Rachel's electrifying renderings made her the Comédie-Française's most valuable asset. In February 1848 Louis-Philippe's monarchy fell, the Second Republic was declared, and the Théâtre Français was renamed the Théâtre de la République. To tap into republican sentiment the director cast Rachel (again playing Camille in *Horace*) in a rousing coda. At the end of the play she wrapped herself in the tricolor, chanted

"La Marseillaise," then fell to her knees in a dramatic collapse. Théophile Gautier reported:

After a few moments the curtain rose again and Camille appeared rid of her Roman robe, straight and tall in a white tunic, and advanced with slow majestic steps to the footlights. We had never seen anything as terrible and thrilling as that entrance and the audience was shivering with fright before the actress delivered a single one of her powerful words. . . . When the actress, like a statue stood firm upon its base, gained her full height, rippled her hips under the full pleat of her long tunic, and raised her arm with a gesture of controlled violence that, with the fall of the sleeve, revealed it bare to the shoulder, then it seemed to everyone that Nemesis, the slow [to rouse] goddess, had suddenly freed herself from a block of Greek marble. . . . Then in an angry voice, both harsh and dull like an alarm-bell, she began the first verse: Allons, enfants de la patrie! *. . . She didn't sing, neither did she recite it, it was a kind of declamation in the style of ancient chants, in which the lines sometimes*

march on feet, sometimes fly on wings, a mysterious music, alien, breaking free of the notes of the composer. . . .[8]

The audience, which had been living under the yoke of the monarchy, exploded with applause for Rachel's donning of the flag of the Republic. As "Liberty leading the people," she was conscious of again rescuing Paris's national theater:

I sang La Marseillaise *only out of devotion, at a more than critical moment, since without it, after all, the Théâtre Français would have perished like so many others in that shipwreck of the revolution.*[9]

The Second Republic lasted a mere four years before Bonaparte's nephew Louis-Napoleon, its president, declared himself Emperor as Napoleon III. In October 1852 Rachel wrote her son Alexandre:

Tomorrow will be the Empire, tomorrow Paris will be bright with lights. I am sorry, my sweet little angel, that you will not be able to help me hang up my lanterns. I am a bit ill, I will unfortunately not be able to go to the Champs-Elysées to see the Emperor's entry into Paris.[10]

Rachel's bouts of coughing and weakness had become chronic, her vis-ible pallor more pronounced. For years she feared an early death from pulmonary consumption, the same disease that killed her great tragedienne predecessor, Adrienne Lecouvreur, whose art she aimed to equal. In 1849 when she acted the part in Scribe's play *Adrienne Lecouvreur,* written for her, she feared it was a rehearsal for her final act. A reviewer wrote:

When at length she expired, and remained with open eyes, with a countenance rigid with death, and with intelligence still written on the features, the effect was most appalling, and a sense of awe seemed to pervade the audience before they broke into the loud applause which once more summoned the great tragic actress.[11]

Though her illness sapped her strength, she wielded her weight as queen of the stage. Choosing only those roles that appealed to her, in 1854 Rachel denied the Empress Eugénie's request for her to perform in *Marie Stuart*, a play in which the director had cast Rachel and her stage rival Mademoiselle Georges as the adversaries Elizabeth Queen of England and Mary Stuart, Queen of Scots, doubly satisfying to knowing audiences.

But Rachel would countenance no peers in her majesty. At the pinnacle of her career she likened herself to Napoleon. In a letter from Brussels to her daughter Adele she announced, "Another nation conquered!"[12] From Russia she wrote that she was received "like a sovereign, not a make-believe sovereign of tragedy, with a crown of gold-colored cardboard, but a real sovereign made by the Mint," and added that her theatrical triumph would compensate for Napoleon's defeat in 1812 when he attempted to lay siege to Moscow: "Moscow will soon be taken; the Muscovites are paying back with interest all they took from us in 1812."[13]

Toward the end of her performing days when she suffered fevers and weakness from advancing tuberculosis, her former Napleonic bravado yielded to the tones of a retreating emperor:

My body and mind have dwindled to nothing. I bring back my routed troops to the banks of the Seine, and perhaps, like another Napoleon, I will go to die at the Invalides and request a stone to lay my head upon.[14]

Instead, the Comédie-Française, deep in her debt, erected in its entry a white marble statue of the fiery actress who became its most famous heroine.

Sites

Comédie-Française
(Théâtre Français)

2, rue de Richelieu (1st arr.)
Tel: 08 25 10 16 80
Métro: Pyramides
Salle Richelieu: Daily 11am to 6pm
www.comedie-francaise.fr

Rachel's sculpture is directly to the left of the entrance inside the theater. Louis XIV had established the Comédie-Française in 1680 to preserve the works of Molière, Racine, and Corneille. Emperor Napoleon, who believed it was "the school for great men," restructured the theater in 1812, and even took lessons in oratory from the great actor, Talma. Today, the government subsidizes one-third of its budget.

Musée du Louvre

(1st arr.)
Tel: 01 40 20 50 50
Métro: Louvre-Rivoli
Daily except Tuesday 9am to 6pm;
Wednesday, Friday until 10pm
www.louvre.fr

Paintings

Jacques-Louis David's *Oath of the Horatii* (1784) portrays the dilemma of the character played by Rachel (Camille) in Corneille's tragedy *Horace*. Horace's three sons are portrayed swearing an oath to their father to fight the Curiaces. Camille (right), Horace's daughter, leans her head on the shoulder of her Curiace sister-in-law, Sabine, who is married to one of Camille's brothers.

Eugène Delacroix's *Liberty Leading the People* represents the July Monarchy Revolution of 1830. Rachel's routine chanting of "La Marseillaise" while wrapped in the flag at the end of her performances during the Second Republic resembled the scene depicted in the painting. Eventually, the painting of "Liberty" (painted in 1831 — Delacroix was witness to the July Monarchy Revolution) came to stand for the Revolution of 1789, not that of 1830.

Residence

9, Place des Vosges (4th arr.)
Métro: St. Paul or Bastille

Rachel rented this apartment shortly before she died.

Gravesite

Division 7, Père Lachaise Cemetery (20th arr.)
Principal entry: 16, rue de Repos
Tel: 01 40 71 75 60
Métro: Philippe Auguste
Generally the cemetery is open Monday–Friday 7:30am to 6pm; Saturday 8:30am to 6pm; Sunday 9am–6pm, 5:30pm November–March, but hours may vary.
www.pere-lachaise.com

Rachel's funeral on January 11, 1858, befitted the queens she played. Six hundred carriages and tens of thousands filled the streets as the hearse passed the Place des Vosges and the Bastille on its way to the cemetery where she is buried in a Greek mausoleum.

 Rachel inspired the characters Vashti in Charlotte Brontë's *Villette* and Miriam Rooth in Henry James's *The Tragic Muse*.

Amantine Aurore Lucile Dupin Dudevant / George Sand

(1804–1876)

NOVELIST, PLAYWRIGHT, AND
CELEBRATED *BOHÈME*

Aurore Dupin Dudevant became George Sand, in Paris in 1832, with the publication of her novel, *Indiana*.

The first Parisian *bohèmes* were no impoverished Rodolfos or Mimis. They were the Théophile Gautiers and Aurore Dudevants who came to Paris with support from bourgeois families. Madame Dudevant, a wealthy heiress in Nohant in the early stages of leaving her faltering marriage to earn a living by her pen, drew a six-month allowance of 3000 francs ($600) from her grudging husband, Casimir Dudevant. Under the Napoleonic Code wives were minors subordinate to husbands who held the purse strings. Over the next forty years Aurore Dudevant would divide her time between Nohant and Paris.

The Paris apartment she rented in 1831 on her modest budget had three small rooms that overlooked the Seine on the Quai Saint-Michel:

I had the sky, the water, the air, the swallows, greenery on the rooftops; I did not feel as if I was in the cultured Paris which was neither to my liking nor resources but in the picturesque or poetic Paris of Victor Hugo, in the old city.[1]

In reality, the Paris of her day was cavernous and dark with five-story houses pitched over alleyways oozing with filth. The following year the narrow streets below would be filled with wagonloads of corpses trundling off to the morgue, as Sand describes:

It was a horrible spectacle. . . . Cholera engulfed first the quartiers that surrounded us; it approached rapidly, it climbed, floor by floor, the house where we lived. It carried off six people and stopped at our mansard door.[2]

A few months later in 1832 as fears of the epidemic waned, fans would mount those same stairs in her pursuit. Her newly published novel *Indiana* had created a sensation: Balzac found it "deliciously conceived," Musset, a "true feeling of suffering and moral turpitude," the *Cabinet de Lecture*, "a declaration of war on the Code Napoleon."[3]

French School (19th century): George Sand

Chawton House Library, Hampshire, UK / The Bridgeman Art Library International

For Parisian women—sixty percent were literate—Indiana's loveless marriage and attraction to her cousin Ralph brought to mind the ill-suited matches endured by many. In its portrayal of the freedom to love whomever one chooses over the chains of arranged marriages, the story became so popular that in faddish imitation Parisian couples signed their love letters "Indiana" and "Ralph."

Sand's own troubled marriage and ensuing love affairs (with Jules Sandeau, Alfred de Musset, Michel de Bourges, Prosper Mérimée, and Marie Dorval, among others) gave rise to characters and plots that explored her predicament and subjected romantic love to close analysis. Praises poured in for *Valentine,* whose incompatible partners were wedded to the same fate as those of *Indiana,* but when *Lélia* hit Paris streets, the press sharpened its pencils. Reviewers were shocked by characters who bared their secret, sexual longings with such disconcerting honesty. They had never encountered a heroine like Lélia, who described in painstaking detail her frustrated desire in her lover Sténio's embrace:

Close to him I felt a strange, delirious eagerness, which originated in the most refined

powers of my intelligence and could not be gratified in a carnal embrace. My breast was consumed by an unquenchable fire and his kisses brought me no relief. I embraced him with a superhuman force and collapsed, totally drained, unable to express to him my burning desire.[4]

Equally disturbing to them was Lélia's courtesan sister Pulchérie, who confessed to having been first awakened to sensual desire by Lélia's beauty:

Your thick, black hair stuck to your forehead and fell in twisting curls as if a life force had contracted them next to your neck, velvet with shadow and perspiration. I passed my fingers through them: it seemed that your hair tightened around my fingers drawing me toward you.[5]

Sand's own amorous relationship with actress Marie Dorval led the press to identify the author with Lélia. Sand claimed that her characters were not meant to be "real persons" but instead personifications of philosophical tendencies; she said Pulchérie was

Antar Teofil Kwiatowski: Frédéric Chopin in concert at the Hôtel Lambert, Paris, 1840

epicureanism and Lélia, nineteenth-century spiritualism. Reviewers' critiques were a double-edged sword: their remarks put off some people but drove up sales among the curious.

Offended readers soon forgave Sand her *Lélia* ways, unable to resist her offerings in the new Paris phenomenon: the serial novel. They devoured each installment and craved its sequel. The *Revue des Deux Mondes* paid her 4,000 francs for thirty-six pages a week for the episodic suspense she whipped off with ease. Subscribers increased from 30,000 to 40,000, until the government suppressed the journals for their dangerous urging to oppose the king's policies.

During the 1830s King Louis-Philippe's liberal market economy left many working-class wage earners in abject living conditions. Stirred up by Eugène Sue's novels that touted socialist policies, disgruntled laborers elected him deputy to the National Assembly in the hopes of action on their behalf. Women's groups angled to do likewise for their own cause by putting Sand in office, but considering herself neither a feminist nor what she wrote propaganda, she refused.

If George Sand's novels were fashioning her image into a proponent of women's causes, her sartorial gear sent gender-bending signals to her fans in the street. New to city life, she felt hampered in women's impractical clothing:

On the Paris sidewalks I was like a boat on ice. Fine shoes cracked in two days, clogs made me fall, I didn't know how to lift my dress. I was covered with muck, tired, cold . . . men, at that time, wore tailored coats, called landowners coats, that came down to the heels. [6]

With coat, trousers, waistcoat, top hat, wool tie, and comfortable boots—a practical and less costly ensemble—she could move with ease, escape attention, go out without a male escort (against the mores of the day) and get down to work:

I could fly from one end of Paris to the other . . . I was neither a lady nor a gentleman . . . I was an atom lost in an immense crowd . . . In Paris, no one thought anything about me, they didn't see me . . . I could write a whole novel from one city limit to the other. . . . That was better than a cell. [7]

She wrote through the night, eight hours or more. During the day there were domestic concerns (her daughter Solange and son Maurice), the acrimo-nious business of separating from Casimir—divorce was illegal and separation nearly impossible—and the next lover to enter her life: Frédéric Chopin.

He was the musical darling of Paris salons. Princesses took lessons at twenty gold francs a session from the composer who hated to play in public and retreated from receptions directly after his recitals. A fragile genius, "not of this world," Chopin was puzzled and seduced by the advances of this "unfeminine woman" who herself had been given a fine education in music. Her simple overture to him came in a note after hearing his *Etudes* one evening at the Hôtel de France: "We adore you. George." [8] Three months into their liaison, she wrote: "If God sent death for me one hour from now, I would not complain at all since these three months have been pure intoxication." [9]

For eight years Chopin and Sand lived as a couple, he often agonizing for six weeks over one measure, she often dashing off thirty pages a night. In 1842 they moved to the New Athens *quartier* where artists settled to flee the city noise. Their apartments in the Square d'Orléans formed a virtual commune with friends: soprano Pauline Viardot, dancer Marie Taglioni, socialist Pierre Leroux, painter Eugène Delacroix, actress Marie Dorval, poets Heinrich Heine and Adam Mickiewicz. In the evenings they dined, read aloud, and played music.

By July 1847 Sand and Chopin had drifted apart—for her, a wound that would never heal: "My heart and body have been bruised by grief. The pain is, I think, incurable."[10] But Sand always found channels out of her depression. This time Parisian events, she said, summoned her attention: "Personal sorrows disappear when public life calls and absorbs us. The Republic is the best of families, 'the people' the best of friends."[11]

"The people" were in revolt because King Louis-Philippe's counselor had suppressed republican reforms that had been promised in 1830. Newspaper sales, town criers, and public gatherings were forbidden in Paris streets. In defiance the people sang of the government massacre of workers in the Marais, intoned "La Marseillaise" everywhere, and held open-air banquets to strategize resistance.

The monarchy's demise in February 1848 quickened Sand's romantic hopes for a Socialist Republic. When the elec-

tions for National Assembly approached, she warned the newly installed President Louis-Napoleon Bonaparte (Napoleon's nephew) in the *Bulletin de la République* that if politicians did not represent their interests, the people would rise up in force. In June the government closed the National Workshops meant to train laborers for public work projects. Unemployment spiked and blood ran in Paris streets. Socialist Armand Barbès called for a new government and for George Sand's appointment as minister of a cabinet that never materialized. To Sand's dismay demonstrators were rounded up to be executed or transported, and in 1852 the Second Empire was declared.

During the years of her socialist politics in Paris, Sand also experimented with a new kind of fiction that sprang from her childhood countryside of Berri and popularized its folklore. The novels were moral tales about pastoral life, as in *La Mare au Diable* (*The Devil's Pond*), with its simple peasants and pond inhabited by evil spirits, or *La Petite Fadette*, about a young woman endowed with mysterious powers. These novels (in the tradition of Virgil's *Georgics,* remembrances of childhood) would remain among her finest work.

But response to Sand's exhausting literary output (more than eighty works) was uneven because in order to support her family and pay the bills, she produced books too quickly to maintain quality. There were, nonetheless, triumphs that reminded her of her adoring public. In 1863 after the performance of her play *Le Marquis de Villemer* at the Odéon Theater, crowds cheered, "*Vive* George Sand!" while her dear friend Gustave Flaubert stood by her side weeping for joy at the scene.

As she toiled away to keep her family afloat, her political expectations for France became more tempered. With the eruption of the Paris Commune in 1871 after the Franco-Prussian War, Sand was sickened by the bloodshed and revolt that recalled the riots of 1848: the torching of the Hôtel de Ville, Palais de Justice, and Tuileries Palace. Writing to Flaubert, whose conservative political views she had begun to share, she said:

This is no time to be sick, old troubadour, no time to grumble. What we've got to do is cough, wipe our noses, get well, and declare that France is mad, humanity stupid, and we ourselves no more than a lot of badly designed and half-bungled animals. . . .[12]

Sand now said that she was willing to wait for a moderate republicanism to slowly evolve. A painful reminder of her impatient opposition to power during the Revolution of 1848, she watched in 1870 the launching of two hot air balloons from a besieged Paris. The names they bore were heroes of 1848: Armand Barbès and George Sand.

Though moved by the homage to her, she had come a long way from the revolutionary Sand of 1848. Spending more time in her Nohant estate, she continued to publish novels in Paris journals, *La Revue des Deux Mondes* and *Le Temps*, welcomed writers like English poets Elizabeth Barrett and Robert Browning and Russian novelist Ivan Turgenev, and carried on endless conversations with Flaubert. Back to her roots in the Berri countryside, the Paris *bohème* seemed closer to the characters in her pastoral novels than to her controversial *Lélia*. She gardened, roamed the woods, and bathed in the Indre river, a habit from her childhood days. Rather than pose a danger to her well-being, she said the ice-cold water sharpened her vision. In her early seventies, the forever regenerate George Sand felt ready to start anew.

Sites

Birthplace
46, rue Meslay (3rd arr.)
Métro: République
The plaque on the building where Sand was born is incorrect. She was the great-granddaughter, not the granddaughter, of the Maréchal de Saxe.

Residences
31, rue de Seine (6th arr.) (plaque)
Métro: Mabillon or Odéon
19, Quai Malaquais (6th arr.) (plaque)
Métro: St. Germain des Prés or Mabillon
25, Quai Saint-Michel (5th arr.)
Métro: St. Michel

Principal Residence
Square d'Orléans (9th arr.)
Métro: St. Georges or Trinité
The entrance into this picturesque square is on rue Taitbout near the intersection of rue Saint-Lazare. George Sand and Frédéric Chopin plaques are on apartments 5 and 9.

Musée de la Vie Romantique
16, rue Chaptal (9th arr.)
Tel: 01 55 31 95 67
Métro: Pigalle or Blanche
Hours: 10am to 6pm, closed Monday.
This nineteenth-century house, in a bucolic setting, the former residence of artist Ary Scheffer, was transformed into a museum dedicated to George Sand and her contemporaries. The collection includes objects related to her life in Paris. One cultish curiosity that catches visitors by surprise is the glass display case which contains plaster casts of Chopin's left hand next to Sand's right arm. Special exhibits focus on the Romantic period in the arts.

✳ *Impromptu*
Director: James Lapine
Cast: Judy Davis, Hugh Grant,
Mandy Patinkin, Bernadette Peters,
Emma Thompson
C.L.G. Films, 1991

✳ "Notorious Woman"
(TV mini-series released by
Masterpiece Theatre)
Director: Waris Hussein
Cast: Rosemary Harris, George
Chakiris, Jeremy Irons, Sinéad
Cusack
BBC, 1974

Sarah Bernhardt

(1844–1923)
ACTRESS OF THE PARIS AND
INTERNATIONAL STAGE WHO CAME
TO BE KNOWN AS "THE DIVINE SARAH"

To the fifteen-year-old Sarah Bernhardt, the suggestion that she go to the Conservatory sounded like a death sentence. When her mother's lover, the Duc de Morny, uttered the words, she remembered learning from the nuns at boarding school that acting "had killed" Rachel, the star of the Comédie-Française. At first Sarah refused, but for a teenage girl whose father had disappeared and whose mother was a courtesan, the choices were limited to the theater or the demi-monde, the class of kept women.

Cocottes like Bernhardt's mother gained status through liaisons with wealthy men. They rode through the Bois de Boulogne in open carriages like high society *mondaines* and were granted favors beyond their class.

One such favor was the Duc de Morny's sponsorship of Bernhardt at the Conservatory of the Théâtre Français, France's national theater company which performed its classical repertoire at the Comédie-Française. There, teachers trained her in poise and elocution and in the stylized gestures of the great actress Rachel. Though Bernhardt's

mediocre debut in Racine's *Iphigénie* did not bode well for her future there, an offstage incident hastened her outright dismissal: when Mademoiselle Nathalie, a snobbish actress of the Comédie-Française, brusquely shoved Sarah's sister Régine out of her way outside the theater, Bernhardt slapped the woman. Immediately demoted, she was fortunate when three weeks later she was hired as an understudy at the less prestigious Théâtre du Gymnase, where roles helped pay the bills but, as she said, "I was neither a success nor a failure. I simply went unnoticed."[1]

Unfortunately, inadequate resources left her prey to *demi-monde* existence, and in 1864 she bore a child from her liaison with the Belgian Prince de Ligne, who did not recognize the son until Bernhardt became famous.

For the next two years she struggled financially while performing *La Biche au Bois* (literally *The Doe in the Park*, but the slang term *biche* referred to kept women) at the Théâtre de la Porte Saint-Martin, until the director of the Odéon Theater agreed to give her a trial run.

Nadar (Gaspard-Félix Tournachon): Sarah Bernhardt in costume, c. 1860
Bibliothèque de L'Arsenal, Paris, France / Giraudon / The Bridgeman Art Library International

Bernhardt said she preferred the Odéon on the Left Bank, with its students, artists, and intellectuals, to the elitist Comédie-Française across the river with its "stiff, gossipy, backbiting world." Open to the less traditional characters of Romantic repertoires, its actors shared her tastes and belonged to the same social class: "Everyone got along, young people came. . . . Often during rehearsals, several of us would go to big dances in the Luxembourg, during the acts where we did not appear."[2]

It took three years for her to gain recognition at the Odéon. She had starred in Racine tragedies, Molière comedies, and George Feydeau's farces, but her role in *Le Passant* as the troubadour Zanetto in love with an aging courtesan established her reputation. The play was staged 140 times in addition to a command performance at the Tuileries Palace for the Emperor Napoleon III. Students showered her with bouquets in the streets and thundering applause in the audience while older subscribers showed more reserve, still clinging to traditional ideas of women's roles on stage.

By then she was so inspired by her craft that she barely noticed such small grumblings. At the Odéon she inhabited a magical place despite its disrepair and "microbes":

. . . it was with profound joy that I scaled the cold and cracked steps toward my dressing room, calling out bonjours as I ran. Then, free of my coat, hat, gloves I bounded onto the stage, happy to be in this infinite darkness... I found nothing more invigorating than this air full of microbes; nothing more gay than this gloom; nothing more luminous than this black night.[3]

In that black night she worked on a style, unique in its intensity, which calibrated every articulation and gesture to accentuate the character's emotion. These exercises in technique were to hasten the moment of inspiration that she called divine *(le dieu venu).* With her growing distinction on a stage that felt like home, it looked as if her time had finally come.

But it had not. On July 19, 1870, her career was suddenly put on hold when Napoleon III declared war on Prussia. Learning that the enemy was advancing toward Paris, Bernhardt requested permission from the Ministry of War to turn the Odéon into a convalescent hospital for wounded soldiers. Her connections brought plentiful supplies to a *quartier* in the thick of the action. One day as she watched the hospital errand boy run to the pharmacy across the street, he was cut down by an exploding shell. The siege lasted from September 1870 till January 28, 1871, when Paris fell to the Prussians.

On May 10, 1871, when the French government signed the armistice that ceded Paris to Prussia, civil war broke out in the city. The Paris Commune, workers from the city districts called *communes*, refused to yield to Prussian occupation and staged an uprising. By the end of the carnage on May 28, 1871, the French National army had quashed the rebellion.

When life returned to normal and the Odéon reopened its doors, Bernhardt's performances drew only halfhearted applause. It took Victor Hugo's *Ruy Blas* in February 1872 to rekindle the embers of her success, an evening that left the playwright kneeling at her feet in gratitude and the audience jubilant. The revolutionary theme of the play coincided with their recently fallen empire and newly declared Third Republic.

With the leverage of fame, Bernhardt decided to return to the Comédie-Française to increase her earnings. The national theater was in a slump and needed a new Rachel, whose sensational performances had restored its falling revenues twenty years earlier. Formerly reprimanded for her impulsive behavior, Bernhardt was now welcomed with open arms: "My success at the Comédie was assured, and the public treated me as a spoiled child. My comrades were a little jealous of me."[4] This time she performed in classical tragedies with a new leading man and lover, Jean Mounet-Sully. Before long the couple became an object of gossip, a fact which the shrewd director Perrin exploited by pairing them in roles to draw crowds.

From then on numerous peaks marked Bernhardt's rise. The first came at the end of 1874 when she performed Rachel's role of Phèdre for the actress's birthday celebration. Two hundred people had to be turned away, so rousing was the event and high the expectations. For most, Bernhardt's performance was strong, but for those who remembered Rachel, she did not measure up.

Sarah Bernhardt as Hamlet in the 1899 production at the Adelphi Theatre

For Bernhardt, pressure brought on stage fright, causing her to speed through her lines and lose control of her pitch. She had the habit of tuning her voice from alto to soprano before making her stage entrance. When stage fright struck she could hit neither end of her range. During another performance, she said of her voice, "Once pitched too high, it was impossible to redescend. I was on my way and could no longer stop myself."[5] She had to continue in that register until the end of the scene when she collapsed with exhaustion.

Acting had introduced her to stage fright early in her career, but as she explained in her memoir, she developed a stategy to overcome it:

I had recourse to my own motto, Quand Même *[even so], and standing in front of the glass gazing into my eyes, I ordered myself to be calm and conquer myself, and my nerves, in a state of confusion, yielded to my brain.*[6]

Georges Clairin: Sarah Bernhardt in the title role of *Theodora*

Private Collection / Archives Charmet / The Bridgeman Art Library International

As she became more savvy, she extemporized during memory lapses. Once in an awkward moment when she left out two hundred lines, she improvised to her addressee (an actress transfixed in terror): "The reason I sent for you, Madame, is that I wished to tell you why I have acted as I have [Bernhardt hesitates], but I have thought it over, and have decided not to tell you today" (she makes a quick exit).[7]

Such gaffes aside, audiences responded with delirium to Bernhardt's extreme acting style. Reviewers described how her exaggerated gestures and tensed body compounded the anguish she projected on stage. In the role of Phèdre, burning with desire, she

. . . rushes into the room trembling and nervous, with struggles which rend and tear and convulse the system (after which) . . . she sprang forward and recoiled again with the movements of a panther, striving, as it seemed to tear from her bosom the heart which stifled her with unholy longings. . . .[8]

When she acted the part of the dying actress in *Adrienne Lecouvreur,* one theater critic said that the cruel agonies of poisoning Lecouvreur suffered made the audience break out in sobs.

Bernhardt performed at the

Comédie-Française until 1880, when conflict with director Perrin drove her across the Channel into the welcoming arms of London audiences. It was a turning point that inspired her to form her own theater company and go on tour. She planned ambitious programs like the one where she acted in twenty-seven plays in twenty-seven days with seven different roles, two of which she learned en route. She performed classical and contemporary plays and challenged her audiences with her male roles such as Hamlet.

Wherever she went her reputation preceded her. When her boat arrived in New York harbor and the press flooded her cabin, she feigned a fainting fit to frighten them off. And when she stepped from her car to walk to the stage door, crowds swarmed to greet her: one woman pinned a diamond broach on her coat, others asked for her to autograph their sleeves, while another woman behind her tried to cut off a lock of Bernhardt's hair as a souvenir.

Back in Paris, some audiences felt cheated by Bernhardt's repertoire. In 1889 a group published a letter in *Le Gaulois* regretting that the decadent characters she played on stage had denied young girls the chance to see her. Not wanting to disappoint loyal fans, she performed *The Trial of Joan of Arc* at the Théâtre de la Porte Saint-Martin, but after a sixteen-week run developed a severe inflammation in her right knee from falling repeatedly to her knees (in prayer) on bare floorboards. It caused her so much pain that years later she had the leg amputated from the knee down.

Sarah Bernhardt never returned to the Comédie-Française. With her own theater company, she toured Europe and the Americas. In London, the writer and critic Lytton Strachey reported on her performance of *Phèdre*:

To hear the words of Phèdre spoken from the mouth of Bernhardt, to watch, in the culminating horror of crime and of remorse, of jealousy, of rage, of desire, and of despair, all the dark forces of destiny crowd down upon that great spirit, when the heavens and the earth reject her, and Hell opens, and the terrific urn of Minos thunders and crashes to the ground—that indeed is to come close to immortality, to plunge shuddering through infinite abysses, and to look, if only for a moment, upon eternal light.[9]

For those stage moments of *le dieu venu* Bernhardt earned the epithet "the Divine Sarah."

Sites

Birthplace
5, rue de l'Ecole de Médecine (6th arr.)
Métro: Odéon
Sarah Bernhardt was born October 22, 1844, illegitimate daughter of a Dutch courtesan and a Frenchman. Sarah rarely saw her father, who died in 1857. She was an inconvenient charge for her mother, who often confided her to the care of an aunt.

Théâtre de la Ville, formerly Théâtre de Sarah Bernhardt
Place du Châtelet (4th arr.)
Métro: Châtelet
During the directorship of her company, Sarah Bernhardt was closely associated with this theater. The Café Sarah Bernhardt, next door, recalls the theater's former name. The other theaters under her directorship were the Théâtre de la Porte Saint-Martin, Théâtre de l'Ambigu, and Théâtre de la Renaissance.

Théâtre de l'Odéon

Place de l'Odéon (6th arr.)
Métro: Odéon

In 1866 Sarah Bernhardt signed a six-year contract with the theater where she established her reputation. Meant to be a new location for the national Théâtre Français, the Odéon received actors from the Comédie-Française in 1782 who then left when the theater came under private ownership after the Revolution in 1789. The Odéon still operates as one of the main theaters in Paris.

Residences

56, boulevard Pereire (17th arr.)
Métro: Wagram

35, rue Fortuny (17th arr.)
Métro: Malesherbes

Statue

Place du Général Catroux (17th arr.)
Métro: Malesherbes

Gravesite

Division 44, Père Lachaise Cemetery (20th arr.)
Principal entry: 16, rue de Repos
Tel: 01 40 71 75 60
Métro: Philippe Auguste
Generally the cemetery is open Monday–Friday 7:30am to 6pm; Saturday 8:30am to 6pm; Sunday 9am–6pm, 5:30pm November–March, but hours may vary.
www.pere-lachaise.com

Camille Claudel

(1864–1943)
SCULPTOR, "ONE OF THE GLORIES OF
FRANCE"

In 1879 sculptor Alfred Boucher told Louis-Prosper Claudel that his daughter Camille had the talent of a *grande artiste* and that he must bring her to Paris to study sculpture. Boucher was visiting the Claudel household in Nogent-sur-Seine when he saw the girl's sculptures of Napoleon, Bismarck, David and Goliath, Oedipus, and Antigone. Having found clay and a kiln built by her grandfather near the family home, she began sculpting at the age of twelve with no training apart from what she could glean from anatomy books. From that time on, she forced friends and family members to pose for her and habitually missed meals to devote herself to her work. After Boucher's visit, Camille's brother Paul wrote, "My sister being strong-willed, succeeded in dragging the whole family to Paris."[1]

When they moved to boulevard du Montparnasse in 1881, Paris was full of opportunities for sculptors. After the Commune of 1871, the Tuileries Palace still lay in ruins, but the spirit of nationalism had spawned State com-missions throughout the city. Along with the new tricolor flag, the emblem of the Third Republic—the bare-breasted Marianne—appeared in squares, parks, and public buildings.

While symbolic women were being enshrined all over the city, real women sculptors, like Camille Claudel, had limited opportunities. The Ecole des Beaux-Arts, on rue Bonaparte, denied them entry, and of the two schools that admitted women, the Académie Colarossi charged the same fee for everyone, but the Académie Julian doubled it for women.

In Paris Alfred Boucher became Claudel's instructor, but when he suddenly had to leave for Rome, he asked the sculptor Auguste Rodin to take his place. Camille Claudel needed little instruction, Rodin discovered, when he saw the eighteen-year-old's sculpture "Old Hélène" in her studio. She and the young English sculptor, Jessie Lipscomb, had rented a ground-floor apartment on rue Notre-Dame-des-Champs where models came to pose for them regularly. The studio was near the

Camille Claudel in an artist's smock

periphery of the city: Montparnasse, not yet an identifiable *quartier*, had wheat fields, pastures for breeding animals, and stables—a rustic locale fit for artist ateliers.

Sculpture was a messy profession of imposing scale, believed unnatural for women. In the studio Camille wore long, bustled dresses, although she had to climb ladders to cut large blocks of stone or to model clay. Women who preferred to wear men's clothes because they were more appropriate for physical work had to get special permission from the Préfecture de Police.

In 1885 Rodin brought Claudel into his atelier as a *practicienne* to enlarge or reduce his maquettes, sculpt the hands and feet of figures for his "Gates of Hell," and make clay model studies for the "Burghers of Calais." Rodin's friend Mathias Morhardt said of Claudel, "Such a gifted being . . . did not need a long initiation."[2] Before long, Morhardt said, she was sculpting stone and marble (a hard material but fragile for its propensity to crack), on which Rodin just chiseled a few marks before signing it—he preferred to model clay. It was common practice for masters to sign the sculptures of artists working in their ateliers. His reputation was growing and his two workshops at 182, rue de

l'Université and boulevard Vaugirard were expanding. Edmond de Goncourt, after a visit at Vaugirard, described it as an

. . . ordinary sculptor's atelier, with walls spattered with plaster, a wretched cast-iron stove, the cold humidity coming from all these things made of wet clay, wrapped with rags, and with all these casts of heads, arms, legs among which two emaciated cats take the form of fantastic griffin effigies.[3]

To apprentice in Rodin's studio was both a privilege and a disadvantage: inspiration from the master left no time for one's own work. This worried Claudel's father, who wanted to see her sculpt for herself.

Since 1883 she had been exhibiting pieces at the annual Salon in the Palais de l'Industrie on the Champs Elysées. Polemicist Octave Mirbeau called the yearly event "a bazaar of mediocrity, a rummage sale of rubbish, a huge fair of miserable failures and impotent self-conceits,"[4] but the Salon was the only showcase for sculptors seeking commissions. In 1890 it moved to the Champ de Mars (where the Eiffel Tower had just been erected) in a spirit of openness to artists not trained in the Academy. Galleries that promoted individual painters were beginning to appear, but

those for sculpture were rare. In 1889 a Monet-Rodin exhibit at the Galerie Georges Petit established Rodin's fame.

By then he and Claudel were deep in a love affair that shaped their work. He introduced her to the art world and consulted her on his projects. The public recognized Claudel as his model (in "Dawn," "Thought," "The Farewell"), and applauded her bust of Rodin at the 1892 Salon. Their mutually inspired works made it seem an ideal partnership—her "Sakountala," his "Eternal Idol;" her "Young Woman with a Sheaf," his "Galatea."

Response to her work was mostly laudatory. Some critics were befuddled by the idea of "a woman having a man's talent." Mirbeau, an admirer, called her, "Something unique, a rebellion against nature, a woman of genius." Others, like Léon Daudet, Gustave Geoffroy, and Mathias Morhardt, saw in her works, respectively: a lyricism, a Florentine attention to the delicacy of human emotion, dream-like qualities of Greek sculpture. In 1892 when Claudel asked the State to commission a marble version of her couple, "The Waltz," the director of the Beaux-Arts sent a representative to view it. Though the quality of the sculpture was "incontestable," he said, the waltzing couple's nudity was offensive and could not be exhibited in public. Would the artist agree to clothe her figures, he asked? Claudel added flowing drapery that in the end emphasized the couple's movement and pathos, but it was cast in bronze, not sculpted in marble.

When it was exhibited, viewers thought it exquisite but mysteriously disturbing. Claudel's brother Paul claimed that only the woman in the sculpture heard the music of the waltz, not her partner. Others thought the whirling couple looked headed for either ecstasy or doom.

Around this time Camille suddenly withdrew from the atelier; Rodin wrote a letter pleading with her to return:

My ferocious friend, my poor head is very sick, and I can't get up any more this morning. . . . Have pity, cruel girl. I can't go on, I can't spend another day without seeing you . . . My dear one I am on my knees facing your beautiful body which I embrace [a perfect description of his sculpture "Eternal Idol"].[5]

The problem was that he, twenty-four years her senior, would not leave his common-law wife, Rose Beuret, and Camille was as uncompromising in life as in art. On-again, off-again, their relationship sputtered to an end after fifteen years.

The final break came when Claudel's "Maturity" appeared at the 1899 Salon. To the gossiping *tout Paris* the meaning of the poses was easy to decipher: a young woman kneeling (Youth), imploring an older man (Middle Age) to stay with her while a sagging, old harpy (Old Age) ushers him away. Incensed to see his private life on display, Rodin blocked the State commission's plan to cast it in bronze, leaving Claudel a thousand francs in debt for the materials.

Claudel began to resent Rodin and accuse him of stealing her ideas and sculptures. Her marble "Clotho," commissioned for the Luxembourg museum event to honor Puvis de Chavannes, disappeared (and has never been found—the one in the Musée Rodin is a plaster version). Illusions of persecution increased her determination to set herself apart from him.

Shut up in her studio at 113, boulevard d'Italie, she created smaller-scale pieces inspired by people in the street. During an interview in March 1905, she said she wished to ennoble the simple clay that came to life in her hands: "My great desire, my ideal, is to put, in all the forms I extract from clay, an idea . . . the idea is not enough; I want to dress it in purple and to crown it in

Camille Claudel at age 14
Banque d'Images, ADAGP / Art Resource, NY

gold."[6] Her marble and jade "Gossips" and onyx and bronze "Wave" astonished critics with their beauty and perfection: "We stop, surprised and delighted in front of this strange work, skillfully executed and of uncommon size."[7]

Despite praise from critics and support from friends—but not enough commissions to pay the bills—by 1905 her suspicions of "Rodin and his gang" had brought her creativity to a halt. (There *were* sculptors plagiarizing works like "Wave" and "Gossips," and she may have had reason to believe that Rodin stole some of her ideas.) After moving to the Quai Bourbon on the

Ile Saint-Louis, she took to smashing her sculptures in fits of despair and doing away with them in mock funeral burials. That same year Charles Morice sounded the alarm in the December 15 *Mercure de France*:

Camille Claudel is a great artist. Some of us have been saying it for a long time . . . Nothing [is] more lamentably unjust than the fate of this truly heroic woman . . . she remains poor and her output is compromised by the precarious conditions of her life. . . . I shout it in the hope that this iniquity end at last . . . the talent of Camille Claudel is one of the glories, at the same time, the shame of our country.

During the following years Claudel's condition did not improve.

In March 1913, shortly after the death of her father, her sole advocate in the family, her brother Paul had her committed to a mental hospital against her will. Paris papers reacted and took up her cause. Editors denounced the 1838 law that enabled her family to confine her in the Ville Evrard Maison de Santé without sufficient reason. The law, which harkened back to the *lettres de cachet* (the king's sealed orders) of the *ancien régime,* was due to be debated before the Senate in the Luxembourg Palace. (A 1990 law meant to remediate that of 1838 now regulates the involuntary psychiatric treatment of individuals.) For Claudel there was no recourse.

In 1920 the hospital's director wrote her mother that, no longer a danger to herself, Camille could leave the institution. Louise-Athanaise, ashamed of her daughter's art and lifestyle, would not allow her to be discharged. After their mother's death, Camille's sister Louise and brother Paul made no effort to free her.

In defiance of her plight, art critics and supporters campaigned for her release and tried to keep her memory alive with articles and sporadic exhibits. In 1934 women artists, in the Salon des femmes artistes modernes, mounted a retrospective of her work. Rodin asked his friend Morhardt to appeal to the Minister of Political and Commercial Business to help her in any way he could, but the family opposed her leaving the institution. She remained there for the rest of her life.

Eleven years before she died Eugène Blot, a valued friend whose gallery represented her work, sent her a heartfelt letter:

I had lost track of you. . . . Into the scheming world of sculpture, Rodin, you, three or four others maybe, had introduced authenticity; this is not forgotten. X. has a souvenir, still astonishing, of your marble of the "Implorer" (cast by me in bronze for the Salon of 1904), that he considers the manifesto of modern sculpture. You were finally "yourself", totally free of Rodin's influence, as great in inspiration as in craft. The first casting of it, enriched by your signature, is one of the masterpieces of my gallery. I never look at it without unspeakable emotion. I see you again [in the figure of the sculpture The Implorer]. The slightly parted lips, the palpitating nostrils, that radiant look, all that cries out for life in what is the most mysterious. With you, we were leaving the world of false appearances for that of thought. What genius! The word is not too strong.[8]

Four years before her death (having been moved to a different hospital in Montdevergues in the Vaucluse because of war) the strong-willed Camille complained to her brother Paul, "They want to force me to sculpt here; seeing that they cannot, they impose all sorts of burdens on me. That will not change my mind, on the contrary."[9]

Camille Claudel left ninety-nine works, some of which form part of the permanent collection of the Rodin Museum on rue de Varennes.

Sites

Claudel family residence

31, boulevard de Port Royal (13th arr.)

Métro: Gobelins

Louis-Prosper Claudel moved the family to Paris so his gifted children could develop their talents: Camille as a sculptor, Paul a poet, and Louise a pianist. Paul became a noted poet-playwright.

Studio of Camille Claudel

117, rue Notre-Dame-des-Champs (6th arr.)

Métro: Vavin

This street was lined with artists' workshops in Claudel's day. Bartholdi's was on rue Vavin and Paul Gauguin's next door to the Académie Colarossi a block away at 10, rue de la Grande Chaumière. After tourists invaded Montmartre, artists moved to cheaper ateliers in Montparnasse.

Studio of Camille Claudel

19, quai de Bourbon (4th arr.)

Métro: Pont Marie

When the expanding city's noise encroached on the rustic atmosphere of her studio at boulevard d'Italie, Claudel moved to 19, Quai de Bourbon on the Ile Saint-Louis, a serene oasis in Paris. The île's spectacular seventeenth-century mansions had fallen into disrepair and had been divided up for rental. In 1910 the Seine overflowed its banks and flooded her studio.

Musée Rodin

79, rue de Varenne (7th arr.)

Tel: 01 44 18 61 10

Métro: Saint François-Xavier or Varenne

Tuesday through Sunday 9:30am to 5:45pm, last entry at 5:15pm, garden closes at 6:45pm (April to September)

Tuesday through Sunday 9:30am to 4:45pm, last entry at 4:15pm, garden closes at 5pm (October to March)

www.musee-rodin.fr

To keep the memory of Claudel alive, Rodin designated one room of his museum to be devoted to her works. Among Claudel's sculptures in the museum are: "Clotho," a tragic, aged female figure who weaves the fate of humans but is entangled in her own flowing drapery; the marble version of "Sakountala;" "The Wave," a nod to Japanese painter Hokusai but with Claudel's touch of impending tragedy; and "Vertumne et Pomone." One cast of "Maturity" is at the Rodin Museum and a second is at the Musée d'Orsay. "The Implorer" was a separate piece which later was incorporated into the group "Maturity."

Camille Claudel: *The Waltz*, 1905

❀ *Camille Claudel*

Director: Bruno Nuytten

Cast: Isabelle Adjani, Gérard Depardieu

Les Films Christian Fechner, 1988

Maria Sklodowska / Marie Curie

(1867–1934)

TWICE WINNER OF THE NOBEL PRIZE, FIRST, WITH PIERRE CURIE, FOR HER WORK ON RADIOACTIVITY, AND SECOND, ALONE, FOR DISCOVERING RADIUM

At noon on November 5, 1906, a crowd gathered outside the gates of the Sorbonne on rue des Ecoles to attend Marie Curie's lecture, the first ever by a woman there. When guards opened the doors, everyone pushed into the physics amphitheater: girls from the Sèvres Ecole Normale squeezed into the front row while members of the press, photographers, fashionably dressed women and men, Polish immigrants, and university students climbed the steps to find a bench or stood in the aisles. At 1:30 sharp Marie Curie walked through the wooden doors to a rousing ovation.

For Curie it was a somber event. In April of that year her husband Pierre had been run down by a carriage on rue Dauphine at the Pont Neuf, and after his death the University gave her his teaching duties, but not his titled chair (which would have brought additional funding for research).

When Maria Sklodowska had stepped off the omnibus on the boulevard St. Germain in 1891, no one noticed her. The Latin Quarter—the quarter of scholars—was male terrain;

the only women who drew attention were those who sat at boul' Mich' cafés gazing amorously at university men. French girls (but, strangely, not foreign ones) were barred from higher education—which surprised Maria Sklodowska, who left Warsaw to study in Paris for the very same reason: Russian occupiers in Poland had closed the university to women. At the Sorbonne she was one of 210 women among nine thousand students, one of two women who earned the *licence ès sciences* in 1893, and one of five, the *licence ès mathématiques* in 1894. In science she graduated first in her class, and in math, second.

Though the university admitted few women, in time of need gender concerns sloughed away. After France's defeat by the Prussians in 1871 in the Franco-Prussian War, the government was determined never again to lag behind in science. While Maria was preparing her *licence* in math, the Society for the Encouragement of National Industry hired her to study the magnetic properties of steel. Her stipend coincided with university efforts to

Valerian Gribayedoff: Marie and Pierre Curie in their laboratory

Collection Kharbine-Tapabor, Paris, France / The Bridgeman Art Library International

update its science program. In 1891 the building on rue des Ecoles looked like a construction site; new laboratories were being added, along with an observatory dome and a tower for physics experiments on falling bodies.

When Maria mentioned to friends her need for more lab space for her research, they introduced her to Pierre Curie, who had some to share. As she wrote,

We began a conversation which soon became friendly. It first concerned certain scientific matters about which I was very glad to be able to ask his opinion. Then we discussed certain social and humanitarian subjects which interested us both. There was, between his conceptions and mine, despite the difference between our native countries, a surprising kinship, no doubt attributable to a certain likeness in the moral atmosphere in which we were both raised. . . .[1]

He was stunned to meet her. By then Pierre had reconciled himself to remaining single, knowing there was slight chance of finding a wife who shared his devotion to science. Love for their work and similar social outlooks welded a special alliance, and they married in July 1895.

Both were outsiders to the science establishment. Marie was a woman of Polish birth, doubly excluding her, and the home-schooled Pierre had not attended the prestigious Ecole normale supérieure that opened doors to prized academic positions. He was teaching at the less notable Ecole municipale de physique et chimie industrielle and had no intention of getting a doctorate. Pierre cared more for his work than accumulating degrees and already his study of crystals and his postulated laws of symmetry, important for the laws of magnetism, were well known. Like Pierre, Marie wanted nothing more than a well-equipped lab and enough funding to continue her work.

After their marriage she began to look for a subject on which to focus her own research. A few years earlier the physicist Henri Becquerel had discovered rays given off by uranium, and Lord Kelvin in England observed how the element and its compounds electrified the air. Marie decided to follow this line of research by measuring the energy given off by the element, a subject in no way as fashionable as X-rays, which monopolized the attention of the scientific community at the time.

Pierre temporarily dropped his own work on crystals to work with Marie.

They built an ionization chamber to measure the energy and while Marie investigated pitchblende for uranium rays, she and Pierre discovered other more active elements. One they named polonium (after Marie's native Pologne) and a few months later discovered radium in active barium. In July 1898, Henri Becquerel read their paper on polonium at the Académie des Sciences — the Curies, not being members, were not allowed to present their research themselves. The Académie awarded Marie Curie the Prix Gegner — 3,800 francs — for this work, which they wanted to encourage. As an insult to her, members did not notify her directly but instead told Pierre.

After their discovery of radium, Pierre turned his attention to understanding radioactivity, while Marie worked at isolating radium. The task would take her three years, laboring in the dilapidated lab on rue l'Homond (location of the Ecole supérieure de physique et chimie), a shed with no ventilation and a small, inefficient stove. All day she stirred large vats of boiling pitchblende, twenty kilos at a

The Curies' laboratory

© Musée Curie (collection ACJC) / Institut Curie

time, with an iron bar as long as she was tall, moving the vats from place to place, and pouring the liquid into other basins. She would then subject the liquid to the delicate process of crystallization, which the coal and iron dust floating about in the air made almost impossible to carry out. Pierre admitted that in her place, he would never have chosen this path, given the lack of support. Marie was happy despite the conditions:

. . . A great tranquility reigned in our poor shabby hangar; occasionally, while observing an operation, we would walk up and down talking of our work, present and future. When we were cold, a cup of hot tea, drunk beside the stove, cheered us. We lived in a preoccupation as complete as that of a dream.[2]

In 1903 the Curies won the Nobel prize with Becquerel for discovering radioactivity. Though the Nobel committee had first omitted Marie's name from the award, Pierre insisted that she be given her due.

While both were exhilarated by their work, they were also frustrated by their poor lab facilities and meager resources. After they won the Nobel prize, journalist Paul Acker of the *Echo*

de Paris reported the conditions under which they had toiled:

Behind the Panthéon, in a small narrow street, dark and deserted, as you'd see in etchings illustrating old and melodramatic novels, the rue l'Homond, between black and cracked houses, at the end of a crumbling sidewalk a miserable wooden shanty stands: it is the Ecole Municipale de Physique et de Chimie [Municipal School of Physics and Chemistry where Pierre taught] . . .

I crossed a courtyard whose lamentable walls had suffered the depredations of weather, under a solitary, vaulted roof where my steps resounded, and found myself in a humid cul-de-sac where between some planks of wood a twisted tree stood. There, some makeshift sheds in a row, low, with small windows where I noticed some short flames and glass instruments. . . . I entered into a laboratory of astounding simplicity: an uneven, dirt floor, poorly plastered walls, an unsound, latticed roof, and daylight that barely penetrated the dust covered windows. . . . It was cold. Water was dripping from a faucet. Two or three gas jets burned. . . .[3]

To get fresh air and exercise after long periods of working with toxic substances, Pierre and Marie would set out on their bikes. Women in "masculine

attire" struck many as unseemly, but Georges Montorgueil predicted the bicycle would liberate them:

The leveling and egalitarian bicycle has created a third sex. This is not a man, this passerby in blousy knickers, calf exposed, torso set free and crowned with a boater . . . Is it a woman? The vigorous step, the lively walk, hands in the pockets, moving about at will and without a companion, settling in on café terraces, legs crossed, speech bold: this is a 'bicycliste.'[4]

Women were liberated, but only a little.

After Pierre died, Marie applied for membership in the Académie des Sciences, which would provide more funding for her work. On January 26, 1911, the Académie convened for a vote at the Institut de France on the Quai de Conti. The choice was between Marie Curie and Edouard Branly for his experiments with radio waves. Throngs of people waited at the entrance as guards kept order and enforced the tradition that no woman enter the hall. Over-eager spectators, once inside, had to wait hours before the vote was taken and the ballots slowly tallied: Branly received thirty votes, Marie Curie twenty-eight.

The press claimed that in requesting membership Curie had overstepped her station, warning that women who engage in men's pursuits "neglect their households," "abdicate their feminine character," and "make men's work disappear."[5]

Supporters rushed to her defense. Gaston Darboux, member the Académie des Sciences and the Faculté des sciences had argued in *Le Temps,* "Now that the moment has come we will not hesitate to defend the cause which appears to us to be just." Marguerite Durand, founder of the feminist paper *La Fronde,* praised Darboux as "one of those who believes that brains have no sex." She wrote that "the principle of masculine supremacy is going to crumble because nothing justifies it in a time when the power of brains is happily more important than muscles." Curie's rejection, she predicted, "will have furnished feminism with one of the most precious pieces of ammunition for its campaigns."[6]

If Marie was able to console herself by remembering Pierre's similar defeat

Marie Curie with daughters Ève and Irène, 1908.

years before — twice denied admittance to the Académie des Sciences — there would be little solace for the next battle.

After Pierre's death Marie had remained in a state of depression for over a year. She wrote in her journal,

It has been a year, I live, for your children [their two daughters Irène and Eve], for your old father. The grief is mute but still there. The burden is heavy on my shoulders. How sweet it would be to go to sleep and not wake up. How young my dear ones are. How tired I feel.[7]

But by 1911 her personal life had taken an upward turn thanks to an amorous liaison with the Curies' old friend, Paul Langevin, who had first comforted her during her long depression. The disclosure of their affair in November 1911 — Langevin was married — became a nightmare.

When journalists caught wind of it, they sided with the wronged wife, Jeanne Langevin, printed lies about Marie and Paul, and pilloried Marie as a foreign threat to the French family. On 5 November 1911, Gustave Téry published the couple's letters found by Jeanne Langevin. Crowds outside Curie's home in Sceaux drove her and her daughters out, and when scientist friends gave her safe haven in their own apartment attached to the Ecole Normale Supérieure d'Ulm (near the Panthéon), government officials pressured them unsuccessfully to make her leave. Langevin, incensed at Téry's action, challenged him to a duel in the Bois de Vincennes on the eastern periphery of Paris, the outcome of which fizzled: Téry could not bring himself to take aim at a man he admired as a great scientist and Langevin lowered his pistol.

It was on 7 November 1911, at the height of this drama, that Marie received the call from Stockholm; she had won a second Nobel prize, this one in chemistry for isolating radium and measuring its atomic weight. But when the head of the committee was notified of the events by the French press, he had second thoughts and told Marie perhaps she should wait until the charges, which were untrue, had been cleared. (Langevin had been accused of consorting with a concubine in the marital dwelling, grounds upon which a wife could file for divorce.) Adamantly, she refused:

The action which you advise would appear to be a grave error on my part. In fact the prize has been awarded for the discovery of Radium and Polonium. I believe that there is no connection between my scientific work and the facts of my private life. . . . I cannot accept the idea in principle that the appreciation of the value of scientific work should be influenced by libel and slander concerning my private life.[8]

Marie Curie was awarded the Nobel prize a second time. Though the scandal exacted a heavy toll on her health, the growing significance of her work was recognized throughout the world and by the end of the decade, her Institut de Radium in Paris gained a prominence unknown to the fossils at the Académie. Today the frequently used unit of radiation is called the *curie*.

Sites

Musée Curie

1, rue Pierre et Marie Curie (5th arr.)
Tel: 01 56 24 55 33
Métro: Place Monge, Cardinal Lemoine;
RER B: Luxembourg
Tuesday to Friday from 10am to 6pm
(except public holidays) Annual closure:
August and last week of December
www.curie.fr

In the museum are Marie Curie's
office and laboratory, and a permanent
exhibit of the instruments used in the
Curies' research. The tour guide likes
to show visitors the now-framed
formula notations on a piece of paper
that is still radioactive.

A few blocks away at 10, rue
Vauquelin is the site of the shed where
the Curies discovered polonium and
radium in 1898. In the courtyard
of the Ecole supérieure de physique
et de chimie industrielles is a plaque
marking the former location of the
shed. Ask the guard at the entrance
gate to direct you to it. The shed was
removed long ago because of its
residual radioactivity.

Académie Française (Institut de France)

23, Quai de Conti (6th arr.)
Tel: 01 44 41 43 00
Métro: Pont Neuf or St.-Michel
www.academie-francaise.fr

On January 4, 1911, for the preliminary
vote on whether or not a woman could
be nominated (much less elected) to
the Académie, twice the usual number
of members showed up for the vote,
160 instead of 70. In attendance were
the Prince of Monaco, Prince Roland
Bonaparte, and Baron Edmond de
Rothschild. *L'Intransigeant* reminded
readers, "Never in memory had there
been such a flood of embroidered
suits [the attire for "academicians"]
under the Cupola."[9] Speeches invoked
tradition: women were barred from
the Institut because the founders never
intended for them to be admitted. And
a woman's election to the Académie
could then lead to the unthinkable:
her nomination for president of the
august body.

Residence

36, Quai de Béthune (4th arr.)
Métro: Pont Marie

Marie Curie moved here in 1912 after
being driven with her daughters from
their home in Sceaux by angry mobs,
following the public disclosure of her
affair with Paul Langevin.

Panthéon

Place du Panthéon (5th arr.)
Métro: Cardinal Lemoine,
RER Luxembourg

On April 20, 1995, President François
Mittérand had the ashes of Marie and
Pierre Curie installed in the Panthéon.
Their daughter, Eve Curie, and Lech
Walesa, the president of Poland,
attended. Marie Curie was the first
woman to join France's *grands hommes*
(the motto on the façade: "Aux Grands
Hommes La Patrie Reconnaissante,"
For Great Men a Grateful Nation).
In the museum crypt, visitors can see
the tombs of the men and woman
interred there.

Sidonie-Gabrielle Colette

(1873–1954)
NOVELIST, WRITER FOR THE STAGE
AND FILM

When Colette arrived as a young bride in Paris in 1893 from a provincial village in Burgundy, she felt a mix of intoxication and despair. There were Montmartre dance halls, *café-concerts*, the cancan at the Moulin Rouge, opium dens, street singers, Maxim's new restaurant. And though Paris monuments were suffused with light, she and her husband Willy (Henri Gauthier-Villars) had moved into a dingy, poorly furnished apartment at 28, rue Jacob on the Left Bank. Willy was fourteen years older, a *boulevardier* writer known about town not only for his articles, but also for so-called collaborations with other writers where he often took credit for their material. Though influenced by her mother Sido (Sidonie Landoy), who believed in the benefits of free love (whether heterosexual or homosexual) and the evils of marriage, Colette found in Paris a world she had never imagined: out to shock bourgeois society, Willy wrote about sadomasochists, necrophiliacs, hermaphrodites, and pornography. But he also introduced Colette to *le tout Paris:* the artists, aris-

tocrats, and journalists who shaped public opinion. In salons she had the thrill of meeting Mallarmé, Debussy, and Proust, but despair set in when Willy infected her with syphilis, the dread disease carried by twenty percent of Paris society in 1895, which made her seriously ill for two years.

She would later describe this transition in life as her passage from childhood in Saint-Sauveur to the loss of innocence in the city. But Colette's states of innocence and experience worked only in tandem, the one shedding light on the other. In the end her adolescent fantasies of sexual games with an older man were destroyed by the ugly experience.

Later in her memoirs she likened her childhood bliss in Burgundy to a life full of roses, but then questioned the value of a rose's beauty without the worm of decay. Colette, the mature writer, had learned that "innocence" needed "knowledge" to shape experience into art and literature.

The young Colette had never aspired to either. It was Willy who encouraged

Colette à quinze ans

her to write about childhood memories in Saint-Sauveur and to include enough spicy details to heighten the flavor. She set about the task—she said Willy had forced her—sitting at her desk eleven hours a day, facing the wall to avoid distractions, and writing volumes, only to cut more than she left in.

The heroine of her first novel *Claudine at School* (1900) was an ostensibly innocent schoolgirl who spun unbridled fantasies and divined villagers' secrets, such as her teachers' lesbian relationships; the adult world seen through the eyes of a child. The *Mercure de France* said *Claudine* was "neither a novel, nor a thesis, nor a manuscript, nothing we've ever known or expected, it is a living person, believable and dreadful."[1] Neither formulaic pulp fiction, nor salacious pornography, it was a roman à clef that thinly veiled the identity of villagers in Colette's hometown, Saint-Sauveur.

By 1903 Colette's *Claudine* series, of which Willy claimed authorship, had become wildly popular. *Claudine at School* sold forty thousand copies in

French photographer: Colette, age 15, 1888

two months; *Claudine Married* went through one hundred printings; *Claudine in Paris* was adapted for the stage. Willy's brilliant promotional skills exploited the success, with Claudine-themed ice cream, perfume, cigarettes, hats, and lotions. He dressed Colette and the popular actress Polaire, who played Claudine on stage, as twins, and posted their pictures everywhere.

Though not high literature, the *Claudine* series was a preview of what would become Colette's literary preoccupations: the themes of love and sensuality in all their nuances. In *Claudine Married* the heroine says: "Vice is the evil one does without pleasure." Instead she prefers rapturous surrender, "To abandon oneself to the intoxication of cherishing and desire—forget all one loved, and start to love over again . . . that's the end of the world."[2] Colette's later works would plumb more deeply the intricacies of love.

In 1910 the not-so-nuanced intricacies of love between Willy and Colette led to divorce. There were infidelities on both sides and, short of money, Willy sold the rights to the *Claudine* enterprise without telling Colette. (After the divorce she signed her novels "Colette Willy," but not until 1924 with

The Hidden Woman did she use solely her surname "Colette.")

By then she had launched her career in music halls and theaters like the Gaieté-Rochechouart. She wooed audiences as a mime, actress, and singer, and shocked them as a dancer in transparent costumes. At the Moulin Rouge, her performance in *The Dream of Egypt* was closed down for indecency by the police, when her lover Missy (the Marquise de Belbeuf), playing a male Egyptologist in love with a resurrected mummy (Colette), kissed her passionately on stage.

Acting and journalism had become important sources of income since her divorce. At *Le Matin* (where she met her next husband, Henry de Jouvenel) Colette contributed two articles a month which included reports on aviation, written from an airbus and a dirigible. As a correspondent during the war, she covered the action in Italy. At the same time, *La Vie Parisienne* published serialized episodes of her new novel *The Vagabond,* which later would be adapted for the stage and for film. Like much of her fiction, its character Renée, on tour as an actress with a theater group, closely reflected Colette's own experiences in music halls and

Colette with Willy
Archives du Centre d'études Colette / Conseil Général de l'Yonne

2057. Paris. - La Gaîté Rochechouart

café-concerts. Renée is a solitary figure, barely communicating with others except for practical reasons. Her motives remain impossible to define: pride, desire for freedom, a restless *ennui*?

Colette liked to claim that her life imitated her fiction. The statement held true for her 1920 novel *Chéri*, the story of a love affair between fifty-year-old courtesan Léa and nineteen-year-old gigolo Fred Peloux (Chéri). Its publication preceded by three years a scandalous affair with her sixteen-year-old stepson, Bertrand, from her second husband, aristocrat Henry de Jouvenel. The couple's divorce followed the next year.

The gossip about Colette and Bertrand that spread throughout Paris circles did nothing to dampen reviewers' praise for *Chéri* as a serious literary milestone. The novel gives weight to maternal and filial longings that fuel the romance between the aging Léa and the young Chéri. After they separate, Léa dwells on the irony of their mutual loss, "My poor Chéri, isn't it funny that in you losing your old, worn out mistress, and in me, my scandalous young

lover, that we have lost what we had that was the most honorable on this earth?"[3] Fernand Vanderem in *La Revue de Paris* wrote that Colette's novel was the most vivid portrait and detailed description ever of the feelings and thoughts of the *demi-monde*. In short, she was indeed a great writer.

When journalist Jean de Pierrefeu severely criticized Colette in *Le Journal des Débats* for wasting her talent on characters he considered to be vulgar and beneath her, she countered by saying that this was her most moral book to date.

The dialogue and power of its drama made it perfect for the stage. Adapted for the theater in 1921, Colette starred as Léa at the Théâtre Daumon in Paris. In 1923 she would play *The Vagabond*'s Renée at the Théâtre de la Renaissance.

During these years, Colette's output was staggering: novels, journalism, performance, even a libretto for Ravel's "Les enfants et les sortilèges" (Children and sorcerers). As a drama critic, she treated plays from the *théâtre du boulevard,* the Folies-Bergère, the circus, and children's theater with the same respect as those of Shakespeare, Racine, and Ibsen. As a film critic, she held film to the same standards as art.

Most important to Colette, she continued to dig into her themes of love and sensuality. Her sensual writing style added to her seductive aura. Men fell in love with her precipitously, as in the case of Maurice Goudeket, who, after discovering her books, declared her to be the only woman who could ever understand him. For ten years they carried on an intimate relationship, and in 1935 they married. He was forty-five and she, sixty-two. As the literary manager of *Paris Match* and *Marie-Claire,* Goudeket would assist her in preparing her voluminous works for a complete edition. He refueled her energies with emotional and financial support, unlike her former husbands, and became a companion in every possible way. From 1939 to 1940, during the German Occupation, Colette and Maurice got up in the middle of the night and drove to rue de Grenelle to do live radio broadcasts to the United States. On the air Colette (who had become an international celebrity) painted a homey picture of French life, its small-town customs and holiday traditions, and spoke of the commonalities between the French and Americans; it was an appeal for help.

When the war ended, Colette was

riding a wave of success and fame. Her last full novel *Julie de Carneilhan* had been published in 1941, but with her novella *Gigi* in 1945 she was elected to the Académie Goncourt. In 1953, a beloved literary figure, she received the medal of Grand Officer of the Legion of Honor. By then visitors descended regularly on the royal *châtelaine* whom physical infirmities had confined to her Palais Royal apartment. Perched at her window on a tuft of cushions, she continued to contemplate the seasonal bloom of the flowers and trees in the park below as she had in her childhood Burgundy garden.

Sites

Residence

93-94, Palais Royal (1st arr.)
Métro: Louvre-Palais Royal
For the last sixteen years of Colette's life she peered out her Palais Royal first-floor window, not far from the small "Place Colette" in front of the Comédie-Française. There she met with Anita Loos to discuss the production of her play, *Gigi,* Jean Marais came to rehearse his part in *Chéri,* and director Jean Cocteau, her neighbor across the garden, came to discuss just about everything.

After Colette was awarded the medal of the Grand Officer of the Legion of Honor, the chef of the two-century-old restaurant beneath her apartment, le Grand Véfour, (www.grand-vefour.com), created a dish in tribute to the grande-dame of sensual pleasure, le Coulibiac de Saumon Colette, her favorite.

Gravesite

Division 4, Père Lachaise Cemetery (20th arr.)
Principal entry: 16, rue de Pepos
Tel: 01 40 71 75 60
Métro: Philippe Auguste
Generally the cemetery is open Monday–Friday 7:30am to 6pm; Saturday 8:30am to 6pm; Sunday 9am–6pm, 5:30pm November–March, but hours may vary.
www.pere-lachaise.com

 Gigi
Director: Vincente Minnelli
Cast: Leslie Caron, Louis Jourdan, Maurice Chevalier, Eva Gabor
MGM, 1958

Colette at the window of her apartment in the Palais Royal

Archives du Centre d'études Colette / Conseil Général de l'Yonne

Gabrielle "Coco" Chanel

(1883–1971)

HAUTE COUTURIÈRE WHO REVOLUTIONIZED TWENTIETH-CENTURY FASHION

Coco Chanel, c. 1930.

Bildarchiv Preussischer Kulturbesitz / Art Resource, NY

Gabrielle Chanel came to Paris in 1909 to open a millinery shop on boulevard Malesherbes with a loan from her lover Etienne Balsan. She had met him while selling hats and doing alterations in a clothing shop in Moulins, where during off hours in the local *café-concert* she tried—unimpressively—to launch herself as a singer (her popular "cock's song," "Ko Ko Ri Ko," may be the origin of her nickname "Coco"). Living with him now in his mansion outside Paris, she hoped again to set out on her own, this time as a milliner.

Though it would be years before she claimed it was her fate to revolutionize fashion, hints of what was to come became apparent during her life among Balsan's friends. Their pastimes—parties and horseback riding—may have bored her to tears, but their wardrobes sparked her imagination and in a spirit of critique prompted her to create her own garments. At the races with Balsan she stood out in the crowd with her simple white collared blouses, navy blue outfits, and streamlined hats, while other women were weighted

down with sartorial coats of mail— whalebone, sable, long dresses, heavy belts, and "*tourte*" pie hats balanced precariously on their heads and speared with long hatpins.

Outgrowing her cramped shop on boulevard Malesherbes by 1910, she opened another in the resort town Deauville where well-to-do customers began clamoring for clothes as well as hats. By 1914 those clients had followed her to the *Chanel Modes* boutique now at 21, rue Cambon in the fashion district of Paris, not far from the Opéra Garnier.

During this time the next man to enter her life, Arthur Capel, introduced her, the product of a Catholic orphanage and boarding school in the provinces, to artists and the influential *tout Paris* where she learned the price of public scrutiny while sharpening her instincts about taste in fashion. The caricaturist Sem, whom Jean Cocteau called a "ferocious insect," affirmed in *Illustrations* that Chanel's designs were *le vrai chic* unlike the gimmicky excesses of other designers, but also sketched a cartoon of her in the embrace of a centaur, Arthur Capel by name. It helped increase her visibility in Paris high fashion, but to her dismay revealed her private life. Among the emerging artists she met was Isadora Duncan, whose dance style and rhythms were meant to convey Eastern philosophies or mythic fantasies. Keen in her observations, Chanel watched with disgust as Duncan performed in her own home on avenue de Villiers, provocatively costumed in a transparent veil (and pawed by a spectator). Gabrielle Chanel had her own ideas about seduction in dress and found Duncan's to be vulgar.

For her, simplicity and nuance were more to the point. Rather than follow the Paris fashion trends of burying women in "feminine" rich velvets, tight, embroidered bodices, frilly lace, knots and pompons, and precious jewels, she chose to set them free in material whose clean lines and fine texture stood on its own merits, an almost austere richness to which she added the fantasies of costume jewelry—strings of pearls or glass beads intertwined with fine, gold chains—no flaunting of wealth with opulent jewels. Seduction was like "reading between the lines," an unen-

cumbered look that by its freshness indicted the old gear that pushed the female form up and out into full busts, squeezed and bruised it with corsets, and tripped it up with full length, flouncy dresses.

At the time in Paris, her rival, Paul Poiret, was designing, for the House of Worth, harem pantaloons, kimono coats, and lampshade tunics that "read well from afar," but Jean Worth, who employed Poiret, was looking up close:

Young Man, you know the Maison Worth . . . possesses the most exalted and richest clientele, but today . . . Princesses take the omnibus, and go on foot in the streets. . . . We are like some great restaurant which would refuse to serve [anything] but truffles. It is therefore, necessary for us to create a department of fried potatoes.[1]

When World War I broke out, Chanel also saw the need for a new vision. Now that their drivers had been mobilized for war, her rich bourgeois clients had to drive themselves, walk, or take the Métro or bus; and she equipped them for shopping in the rain. Inspired by fishermen she had seen on the Normandy coast in Deauville, she introduced rubberized raincoats in blue, black, pink, and white,

with deep pockets and buttons for easy fastening—until then, buttons on women's fashions were often numerous, decorative, and fussy.

Since fabrics were expensive during the war, she ordered the less costly jersey for her dresses. The manufacturer Rodier thought she had taken leave of her senses: jersey for haute couture. At the time, jersey was used only for underclothes. Rodier knew the material would pucker in dresses gathered at the waist. Chanel saw the problem too and accommodated the fabric by designing straight, loose-fitting jackets.

Chanel's fabrics and combinations were unheard of in haute couture. Avoiding the ostentatious display of mink and sable, she used fur only to line and edge her dresses, and even that with the more pedestrian rabbit, mole, and beaver. Straight dresses she softened with extra fabric or flowing scarves around the hips; safari jackets offered pockets for practicality; shortened skirts and looser fits allowed free movement. Parisian fashion magazines such as *Vogue* filled their pages with her styles: bell-shaped hats and caps that spread like wildfire throughout France; waistbands that dropped below the hips; compressed contours that accentuated the vertical line unlike the earlier S-shaped profile with bust protruding and gathered bustle behind. From Russian immigrants, mostly aristocrats who poured into France during the Russian Revolution, Chanel culled other designs, adding expensive embroidered folkloric patterns and colors to smocks and peasant-style blouses, and on neutral black or brown crêpe dresses she splashed patterns of colorful glass beads, sequins, and spangles.

By the end of World War I Coco (the nickname was now used) had not only won over women with her comfortable fashions, but had also developed acute marketing skills. In 1922 Jean Cocteau staged his *Antigone* in the small Atelier theater in Montmartre and engaged Chanel to design the costumes, Picasso to create the décor, Arthur Honegger to compose the music, and Man Ray to take photos. It was a big media event well-timed for Chanel, who draped Antigone in an antique Greek gown similar to the new line she had just launched (a Greek sculpture had also been placed in the entry of her boutique), and bound Creon's forehead in a goldsmith's band studded with imitation jewels—that year her *faux bijoux* (costume jewelry)

made its debut. When the press asked Cocteau why he had engaged Chanel for the costumes, he replied that she she was the greatest *couturière* of the time, and that Oedipus's daughters must not be badly dressed.

Similarly, she introduced her Chanel No. 5 perfume in a sleek, square, beveled bottle with rounded edges—striking in its simple shape—not with great fanfare, but by discreetly offering bottles as gifts to her well-connected friends.

The same year a titillating novel hit the Paris bookstores that brought Chanel even more attention. *La Garçonne* (*The Bachelorette*) told of a young socialite who, having descended into the dark underworld of drugs and orgies, is extricated from her dissolute life by the love of a man who (coincidentally) believes in women's rights. In a fortuitous leap, the media linked the androgynous features of Chanel's styles with the heroine's newfound independence.

Her signature designs originated with what she herself could wear well. Neither buxom nor corset-curved, she did away with belted waists, full busts, and frou-frou flounces. Parisiennes already sported clothes *avec désinvolture*—with nonchalance—to appear as

if they paid little attention to their dress. Now to be both stylish and "liberated" Paris women slimmed down and cut their hair—Coco had done so herself years earlier—as husbands moaned and coiffeurs all over town cheerfully clipped away.

Practical elegance had become Coco's trademark, and everywhere she went, her imagination was sparked by her surroundings. One evening in 1926 during a première at the Opéra Garnier, she peered over the balcony at the audience below and said she was struck by the sight of women "disguised" in Paul Poiret's fashions. He had already accused her of dressing women like "little, undernourished telegraph operators." Now a flash of inspiration gave birth to the *petite robe noire passepartout,* the little black crêpe de Chine dress with its plain round, collarless neckline, dropped waist, fitted sleeves, and soft, pleated skirt. When criticized for its simplicity, she replied by comparing the design of her dress to the clean lines of an airplane.

By the 1930s her friends numbered among the famous artists of the day, and included Igor Stravinsky, Picasso, Salvador Dalí, Sergei Diaghilev, Max Jacob, Jean Cocteau, and Pierre

Reverdy. While listening to them talk about the problems their arts presented, she began to think of her creative decisions in a similar vein, though never called herself an artist.

But why not? In her fourth-floor studio above the boutique—she had moved it to 31, rue Cambon behind the Ritz hotel where she lived—fabrics in colorful palettes and varied textures lay strewn everywhere: rolls and cylinders of tulle, satin, jersey, and crêpe draped across chairs and covering the carpet. She had designed costumes for the theater and films like Jean Renoir's *Rules of the Game*. In 1937 she exhibited her collection at the Universal Exposition on the runway at the Pavillon d'Elégance.

Not long after, when the Nazis occupied Paris, Coco closed her shop. For her, this was no time for haute couture. After the Liberation, her boutique remained quiet for another nine years, most probably for the shame she felt at having had an affair with a German officer, Hans Gunther von Dinklage, during the Occupation. In the meantime her perfume sales were modest, despite a temporary boost when Marilyn Monroe claimed to wear nothing more to bed than a few drops of Chanel No. 5.

In 1947 Christian Dior introduced his New Look, a recycling of Belle Epoque cinched waists, corsets, whalebone, and long skirts. Fashion reviews were ecstatic, but Chanel could not bear to watch women retreat to old instruments of torture. She said that couturiers had forgotten about the women inside their dresses. Dior didn't dress women, she said, but wallpapered and covered them with tapestries to look like Louis XIV armchairs.

Fourteen years after closing her shop, at the age of seventy-one, she went back to work because, she said, she found it difficult to remain idle. On February 5, 1954, the day of her debut fashion show, reviewers wrote her off before they arrived at rue Cambon. Coco stood at the top of the stairway (the beveled mirror along side it hid her from those below while she could see them) as thirty models walked down the runway in an icy silence which Franco Zeffirelli described as the cruelest event he had ever witnessed. Journalists said she brought back the ghosts of the past, outmoded styles of the '30s.

Unfazed, Coco Chanel returned to the drawing board. She reworked her earlier styles and introduced her classic suit in shantung, jersey, and tweed, lined with soft, netting fabric. The collarless, square, short jacket had patch pockets and braided trim; a gold chain in its hem to make sure it hung straight with movement; buttons resembling coins or decorated with gold, interlocking CCs for Coco Chanel; all coordinated with a slim skirt that fell just below the knee. The new suit met with immediate success for its comfort, elegance, and prospects to remain in style for more than one season.

Tired of managing the Chanel enterprise, she sold it in 1954 with an agreement to retain for herself an income from the perfume and to maintain her position in the *maison de couture* as designer.

Chanel's final coup was to cede the rights to her couture lines to American manufacturers to mass reproduce them, resigning from the Paris Syndicate of Haute Couture since her action violated its rules. Her styles were copied throughout the world without her approval, but to her "*La copie c'est l'amour*" (To copy is to love). Christian Dior's New Look, less easy to produce on a large scale, fell out of favor, and by 1957 Chanel was back.

In the end Dior conceded that Chanel revolutionized fashion with a black pullover and ten rows of pearls.

Sites

Maison Chanel

31, rue Cambon (1st arr.)
Tel: 01 42 86 26 00
Métro: Madeleine
Monday through Saturday, 10am to 7pm

To the right of the entrance of the shop you can see the elegant, mirrored stairway Chanel's models descended for her fashion shows. The first floor was Chanel's boutique, the second, her business office, and the fourth, her designer studio. In France, to merit the title of *maison de haute couture* the designer had to satisfy specific criteria: to employ a requisite number of workers, to participate in a significant number of fashion shows, and to use a certain volume of fabric.

Chanel's fashions were revolutionary in replacing the corset with comfortable and elegant styles: cardigans, trousers, the little black dress, costume jewelry, the tweed suit, and buttons that fastened with ease.

Since the early '80s the Chanel designer Karl Lagerfeld has incorporated modern designs with classic Chanel lines. The average cost of a Chanel suit today is $5,000.

Her jewelry boutique is at 18, Place Vendôme directly across from the Hôtel Ritz where her apartment was renamed "Suite Coco Chanel."

✳ ***Coco Avant Chanel***
Director: Anne Fontaine
Cast: Audrey Tautou, Alessandro Nivola
Cine @, 2009

✳ ***Coco Chanel***
Director: Christian Duguay
Cast: Shirley MacLaine, Malcolm McDowell
Lux Vide, 2008
Lifetime biopic.

Simone de Beauvoir

(1908–1986)

PHILOSOPHER, WRITER, FOUNDER OF
THE WOMEN'S LIBERATION MOVEMENT
IN FRANCE

Simone de Beauvoir, author of feminism's groundbreaking book, *The Second Sex,* and symbol of Paris's Left Bank culture, told an interviewer late in life that she would have been

. . . surprised and even irritated if, when I was thirty, someone had told me that I would be concerning myself with feminine problems and that my most serious public would be made up of women.[1]

Until her late thirties she never even considered the topic, having spent her adult life until then in close partnership with philosopher Jean-Paul Sartre and identifying with male intellectuals. Though she could not have escaped society's inequities between men and women, she claimed never to have consciously registered them.

Beauvoir had the luck to be born when, through extraordinary intelligence and drive (her nickname was Castor, the beaver), she could at least finesse, if not contest, obstacles posed to women. Before 1924 the grueling *agrégation,* or teacher exam, in philosophy was closed to women. Beauvoir

and Sartre took the exam in 1929 after meeting at the Sorbonne the year before. Sartre and she ranked first and second, respectively, among the examinees, but he had the advantage of being prepared at the prestigious Ecole Normale Supérieure d'Ulm near the Panthéon, which did not admit females. Beauvoir took courses at Sainte-Marie in Neuilly and the Sorbonne. Sartre studied for seven years to pass, Beauvoir for three.

Sartre and Beauvoir had become a couple by the 1930s, flouting convention by rejecting bourgeois marriage, and vowing an essential loyalty to each other, no matter their contingent affairs. For fifty years they would advise each other about their work, every day meeting, or speaking on the phone, or working six to ten hours in Left Bank cafés at separate tables.

(Sartre and Beauvoir were eventually compared to the famed medieval couple, Abélard and Héloïse. By a strange coincidence Beauvoir was a descendant of philosopher Guillaume de Champeaux, Abélard's competitor

Henri Cartier-Bresson: Simone de Beauvoir, Paris, 1945
© Henri Cartier-Bresson / Magnum Photos

at the twelfth-century Cathedral School of Paris.)

Until the German Occupation Beauvoir wrote at the café Le Dôme in Montparnasse. In the frigid January of 1941 she left for the warmth of the Café Flore near Saint-Germain-des-Prés where she sat upstairs, close to the stove: "We had no coal, my room was not heated; I slept with ski pants and a sweater, between ice-cold sheets."[2] In Paris, where people received rations for a daily diet of 850 calories, the hunger was felt worse than in the countryside, and the death toll rose because of tuberculosis and malnutrition. Theaters and cinemas were taken over by the Germans, restaurants and cafés (the Dôme, Rotonde, Coupole, and Flore) became German haunts, and the city clocks were set to Berlin time.

During the war when Sartre was called up for military service, Beauvoir finished her first successful novel *She Came to Stay*, read and critiqued Sartre's manuscript for his short story collection *The Wall*—he never published anything without submitting it to her editorial eye—and taught philosophy at the Lycée Molière in the sixteenth arrondissement. Examining the jealousy of characters caught in a lover's triangle, *She Came to Stay* brought to life Beauvoir's metaphysical probings of Self and Other: the individual consciousness that sees itself as an "absolute" requiring the obliteration of the other. These questions, which also preoccupied Sartre, would be central to her argument in *The Second Sex*.

By the late 1940s "existentialism," a word adopted by Beauvoir and Sartre, was on everyone's lips. In the aftermath of the war the old moral order had proven hypocritical—for one, how could France have collaborated with the Nazis in rounding up Jews?—and Sartre's philosophy offered something new: in a world without absolutes one was free to create oneself. Young people carried Sartre's *Being and Nothingness* around like a badge and hung out in the subterranean clubs of Le Tabou, Le Mabillon, and other Saint-Germain nightspots.

In 1947 after Beauvoir had published her own book on existentialism, *The Ethics of Ambiguity,* she decided to write a memoir. Quite unexpectedly, she said,

I found that the first question that came up was: of what significance was it to be a woman? I thought I could quickly extricate myself from the question. I never had any feelings of inferiority . . . [but later] I had a revelation: this world was a masculine world, my childhood had been nourished by myths forged by men. . . .[3]

At forty her eyes were opened, and instead of a memoir she wrote *The Second Sex.*

Beauvoir called women the second sex because the male tradition of thought held man to be the Norm and woman the Other; man was X, she was non-X, not an entity of her own but always the negative of the male. According to patriarchal history, woman "in her nature" was a flawed being, lacking man's qualities (Aristotle), an imperfect man (theologian Thomas Aquinas), a castrated man (Freud). Beauvoir observed that woman and man are products of culture like the trimmed trees at Versailles that only *appear* to grow naturally. Her argument that women were not biologically determined by nature but pruned by the "shears" of culture to be the inferior sex rested on evidence she provided from anthropology, history, physiology, and psychology. "One is not born a 'woman,' but becomes one," she said.

On June 18, 1949, she was sitting

on the terrace of the Café Flore when Sartre stopped by to tell her the good news: the first volume of *The Second Sex,* "Facts and Myths," had sold more than twenty thousand copies in the first week and the publisher, Gallimard, could not stock the bookshelves fast enough.

When volume two, "Woman's Life Today," came out in November, it was third on the bestseller list but caused an uproar. Beauvoir's analysis of the origins of women's inferior position in patriarchal society undermined sacrosanct beliefs. Gallimard was suing bookshop owners who banned it; incensed husbands wanted to keep it from their wives; the Catholic Church put it on the Index for its insidious "poison." François Mauriac called it pornography in *Le Figaro*; and the Communist Party claimed it to be of no interest to women workers. In November, when crowds recognized Beauvoir at Les Deux Magots, they mocked her and jeered, shouting obscenities.

But in fact reader reaction was more mixed. Women ripe for its message were dumbstruck. Beauvoir had read their minds, understood their experiences. They felt relief and anger; now they could articulate something they previously could not name. Though some reviled her for threatening their secure places in the home and society—to question them left these women adrift with no psychological anchors—others thanked her: "Your book was a great help to me. Your book saved my life."[4]

It would take twenty years for her ideas to percolate and lead to a full-blown women's movement.

During the interim her output was prolific. She wrote two memoirs (she would write more) and more novels and essays. With Sartre she served as editor of the journal, *Les Temps modernes*, and signed a manifesto against France's war in Algeria (after which they had to hide in strangers' apartments to escape death threats—Sartre's apartment on rue Bonaparte had been partially destroyed by two bombs). In a 1960 article in *Le Monde* she launched a public case in defense of an Algerian woman, Djamila Boupacha, who had been arrested, tortured, and raped by French army interrogators for her role in the resistance during Algeria's fight for independence.

In May 1968 when riots broke out at the University in Paris, Beauvoir and Sartre served as icons of protest. Students called for an overhaul of education: it was antiquated, paternalistic, and out of reach financially for many. Demonstrators built barricades on boulevard Saint-Michel and rue Victor Cousin and occupied the Sorbonne on rue des Ecoles. After the uprising was stanched on May 30th, women who had marched were furious; rather than give speeches and share the leadership with men, they had been relegated to subservient tasks such as typing and making coffee.

Inspired by Beauvoir, women began to organize actions that would publicize their cause. On August 28, 1969, eight women went to the Arc de Triomphe and placed flowers on the tomb of what they called the widow of the unknown soldier, a symbol of the women whose service to the nation was lost to history. It drew media attention and the wrath of veterans.

Next, in Beauvoir's Montparnasse apartment on rue Schoelcher, a group of women devised a strategy to publicly decry the illegality of abortion. They wrote a Manifesto which was signed by 343 women who claimed to have had abortions. On April 4, 1971, *Le Nouvel Observateur* published the Manifesto and created a scandal. The taboo word "abortion" was "outed" in reports everywhere: in the newspapers, on TV, and the radio. Later Beauvoir took to the Paris streets with throngs of demonstrators to demand the legalization of abortion, granted in 1975 by the Veil law. By then *The Second Sex* had become a point of reference for women. That same year during a TV interview Jean-Louis Servan-Schreiber repeated complaints of male critics who contested Beauvoir's authority to write about motherhood, not being a mother herself. Her simple response was like a bullet that hit its mark: "But *they* can?" In 1984 Josée Dayan's documentary on *The Second Sex* was aired on French TV in four hour-long segments despite male producers' demand to cut scenes they found disturbing, like the filming of Arab girls' clitoridectomies.

Though Beauvoir could take pleasure in the changes brought about by feminist activism during the last decade of her life, she was disappointed to see the emergence of a hostile faction of Parisian feminists in the '70s, "Psych et Po" (psychology and politics), who she feared were propounding once again the "biologically determined essence" of men and women. The group, whose prominent spokeswoman was Antoinette Fouque and whose theories were not rooted in existentialism, accused her of denying the difference between men and women. She responded by reminding them that gender difference was cultural, not natural, a theory in keeping with her philosophical understanding that "the human being is an idea, not a species."

With age Simone de Beauvoir became more radical in her efforts to improve women's lot. On April 19, 1986, when thousands gathered at her Montparnasse gravesite the day of her burial, Elisabeth Badinter called her "the mother of us all" and reminded the women in the crowd, "Women, you owe her everything."

Beauvoir herself might have added the comment she made thirteen years earlier to the young Fulbright scholar Alice Jardine, who nervously interviewed the towering figure of feminism at rue Schoelcher:

"If men and women had equal rights, this world would be turned upside down."[5]

Sites

Birthplace

105, boulevard du Montparnasse (6th arr.)
Métro: Vavin

Simone de Beauvoir was born above La Rotonde, where she sometimes worked. In the early seventeenth century a mound of debris — plaster, stones, rubbish — stood at the crossroads of today's boulevards du Montparnasse and Raspail. Students humorously named it Mont Parnasse, the mountain of the gods. It was razed in 1725, but the name remained.

Les Deux Magots

6, Place Saint-Germain-des-Près (6th arr.)
Tel: 01 45 48 55 25
Métro: St.-Germain-des-Prés
www.lesdeuxmagots.fr
Daily 8am to 2am, closed second week of January

Inside the café are two plaques for Simone de Beauvoir and Jean-Paul Sartre at the seats where they worked. The statues of two *magots* (magi, or Confucian wise men) date from 1885. Among those who met there were Mallarmé, Merleau-Ponty, André Gide,

Jean Giraudoux, Picasso, Fernand Léger, Prévert, Camus, and André Breton.

Café Flore

172, boulevard Saint-Germain (6th arr.)
Tel: 01 45 48 55 26
Métro: St.-Germain-des-Prés
Daily 7am to 1:30am
The café opened in 1887 and took its name from the sculpture of a small divinity on the other side of the boulevard. Intellectuals and artists gathered there as well.

Le Dôme

108, boulevard du Montparnasse (14th arr.)
Tel: 01 43 35 25 81
Métro: Vavin
Daily 8am to 1am
As Montparnasse evolved into a popular *quartier*, Le Dôme, La Rotonde, and La Coupole further west on the boulevard drew a clientele of writers, poets, artists, and intellectuals.

Residence

11 *bis*, rue Schoelcher (14th arr.)
Métro: Denfert Rochereau
From her apartment in this beautiful building (marked by a plaque),

Beauvoir had a view of the cemetery of Montparnasse where she and Sartre would be buried.

Gravesite

Division 20, Montparnasse Cemetery
3, boulevard Edgar Quinet (14th arr.)
Métro: Raspail or Edgar Quinet
Hours: Monday through Friday 8am to 5:30pm, Saturday 8:30am to 5:30pm, Sunday 9am to 5:30pm.
Beauvoir is buried next to Sartre.

✳ *Milou en mai* (May Fools)
Director: Louis Malle
Cast: Miou-Miou, Michel Piccoli
Nouvelles Éditions de Films, 1990
Film about May '68 in Paris.

✳ *Paris, je t'aime*
Victoires International, 2006
A whiff of Beauvoir and Sartre: In this film eighteen directors each made one five-minute vignette, each about a different arrondissement in Paris—two were not included. The one shot in the 6th arrondissement is an allusion to Beauvoir and Sartre—often missed by film critics. The directors of that vignette are Gérard Départieu and Fred Auburtin, who also star in it as the waiters; Ben Gazzara and Gena Rowlands play the couple.

ENDNOTES

Geneviève

1. Sévigné, Marie de Rabutin-Chantal, marquise de, [July 19, 1675], Correspondance. Tome 1, 1646–1675 (Paris: Gallimard, 1972), author's trans.

Héloïse

1. Betty Radice, trans., *The Letters of Abelard and Heloise* (London: Penguin, 1974), 66. Reproduced by permission of Penguin Books, Ltd.

2. Constant J. Mews, *The Lost Love Letters of Heloise and Abelard* (New York: Palgrave MacMillan, 2001), 225. Reproduced with permission of Palgrave MacMillan.

3. Ibid., 233.

4. Ibid., 211.

5. Radice, 115.

6. Ibid., 75.

7. Ibid., 113, 116–117.

8. Ibid., 277, 280–281.

Christine de Pizan

1. Charity Cannon Willard, edit., "Christine's Vision" in *The Writings of Christine de Pizan* (New York: Persea Books, 1994), 16. Reprinted with permission of the publisher.

2. Ibid., 17–18.

3. Christine de Pizan, *The Book of the City of Ladies*, Earl Jeffrey Richards, trans. (New York: Persea Books, 1982), 85. Reprinted with permission of the publisher.

4. Willard, 85.

5. Willard, 236.

6. Christine de Pizan, 5.

Marie de Rabutin-Chantal, Marquise de Sévigné

1. Sévigné, Marie de Rabutin-Chantal, marquise de, [June 17, 1687], Correspondance. Tome 3, 1680–1696 (Paris: Gallimard, 1978), author's trans.

2. Sévigné, Marie de Rabutin-Chantal, marquise de, [July 12, 1690], Correspondance. Tome 3, 1680–1696 (Paris: Gallimard, 1978), author's trans.

3. Sévigné, Marie de Rabutin-Chantal, marquise de, [October 7, 1677], Correspondance. Tome 2, 1675–1680 (Paris, Gallimard, 1974), author's trans.

4. Sévigné, Marie de Rabutin-Chantal, marquise de, [July 17, 1676], Correspondance. Tome 2, 1675–1680 (Paris, Gallimard, 1974), author's trans.

5. Sévigné, Marie de Rabutin-Chantal, marquise de, [September 30, 1676], Correspondance. Tome 2, 1675–1680 (Paris, Gallimard, 1974), author's trans.

6. Sévigné, Marie de Rabutin-Chantal, marquise de, [April 24, 1671] Correspondance. Tome 1, 1646–1675 (Paris, Gallimard, 1972), author's trans.

7. Madame de Sévigné, *Lettres* (Paris: Flammarion, 1976), 357–358, author's trans.

8. Sévigné, Marie de Rabutin-Chantal, marquise de, [October 1678], Correspondance. Tome 2, 1675–1680 (Paris, Gallimard, 1974), author's trans.

9. Sévigné, Marie de Rabutin-Chantal, marquise de, [October 11, 1661] Correspondance. Tome 1, 1646–1675 (Paris, Gallimard, 1972), author's trans.

10. Sévigné, Marie de Rabutin-Chantal, marquise de, [February 15, 1690], Correspondance. Tome 3, 1680–1696 (Paris, Gallimard, 1978), author's trans.

Françoise d'Aubigné, Madame de Maintenon

1. Sévigné, Marie de Rabutin-Chantal, marquise de, [December, 1673] Correspondance. Tome 1, 1646-1675 (Paris, Gallimard, 1972), author's trans.

2. Sévigné, Marie de Rabutin-Chantal, marquise de, [September 8, 1676], Correspondance. Tome 2, 1675–1680 (Paris, Gallimard, 1974), author's trans.

3. Sévigné, Marie de Rabutin-Chantal, marquise de, [June, 1680], Correspondance. Tome 2, 1675–1680 (Paris, Gallimard, 1974), author's trans.

Gabrielle Emilie Le Tonnelier de Breteuil, Madame du Châtelet

1. Elisabeth Badinter, *Emilie, Emilie* (Paris: Flammarion, 1983), 177, author's trans.

2. Nancy Mitford, *Voltaire in Love* (New York: Carroll & Graf Publishers, Inc., 1999), 145.

© Nancy Mitford. Reproduced by permission of the author's estate c/o Rogers, Coleridge & White Ltd., 20 Powis Mews, London W11 1JN.

3. Badinter, 87, author's trans.

4. Mitford, 80-81.

5. Badinter, 325–326, author's trans.

6. Ibid., 330.

7. Mitford, 271.

8. Esther Ehrman, *Mme du Châtelet* (Oxford: Oxford University Press, 1986), 84, 88. By permission of Oxford University Press, Inc.

9. Badinter, 319–320, author's trans.

Marie-Jeanne (Manon) Phlipon, Madame Roland

1. Simon Schama, *Citizens, a Chronicle of the French Revolution* (New York: Vintage Books), 605. Reprinted with permission of the publisher.

2. Gita May, *Madame Roland and the Age of the Revolution* (New York: Columbia University Press, 1970), 218. Reprinted with permission of the publisher.

Elisabeth Vigée Le Brun

1. Elisabeth Vigée Le Brun, *Souvenirs I* (Paris: Éditions Des Femmes: 1986), 138, author's trans.

2. Ibid., 37.

3. Ibid., 77.

4. Mary D. Sheriff, *The Exceptional Woman* (Chicago: University of Chicago Press,

1996), 128. Reprinted with permission of the publisher.

5. Elisabeth Vigée Le Brun, *Souvenirs II* (Paris: Éditions Des Femmes, 1986), 79, author's trans.

6. *Souvenirs I*, 56.

7. *Souvenirs II*, 159.

8. Ibid., 214.

Eliza Rachel Félix

1. Rachel Brownstein, *Tragic Muse* (New York: Knopf, 1993), 95. Reprinted with permission of the publisher.

2. Theophile Gautier, *Victor Hugo* (Paris: Charpentier, 1902), 18–19, author's trans.

3. Brownstein, 103.

4. Ibid., 171.

5. Ibid., 121.

6. Francis Gribble, *Rachel, Her Stage Life and Her Real Life* (London: Chapman and Hall, Ltd., 1911), 63.

7. Michael Booth, John Stokes, Susan Bassnett, *Three Tragic Actresses* (Cambridge University Press, 1996), 100. Reprinted with permission of Cambridge University Press.

8. Ibid., 110–111.

9. Ibid., 192.

10. Ibid., 192.

11. Ibid., 106.

12. Brownstein, 197.

13. Ibid., 200.

14. Ibid., 209.

Amantine Aurore Lucile Dupin Dudevant / George Sand

1. Huguette Bouchardeau, *George Sand* (Paris: Robert Laffront, 1990), 69, author's trans.

2. Hortense Dufour, *George Sand, la somnambule* (Monaco: Rocher, 2002), 262, author's trans.

3. Ibid., 264.

4. George Sand, *Lélia*, author's trans.

5. Ibid.

6. Bouchardeau, 70-71, author's trans.

7. Dufour, 407, author's trans.

8. Ibid., 415.

9. André Maurois, trans. Gerard Hopkins, *Lélia, the Life of George Sand* (New York: Harper, 1953), 331. Reprinted with permission of HarperCollins Publishers.

10. Dufour, 463, author's trans.

11. Maurois, 451.

12. Dufour, 472, author's trans.

Sarah Bernhardt

1. Arthur Gold and Robert Fizdale, *The Divine Sarah* (New York: Knopf, 1991), 58. Reprinted with permission of the publisher.

2. Sarah Bernhardt, *Ma Double Vie I* (Paris: Edition Des Femmes, 1980), 189, author's trans.

3. Ibid., 190.

4. Sarah Bernhardt, *Memories of my life,* (New York: D. Appleton and Company, 1907), 239.

5. *Ma Double Vie I*, 127.

6. *Memories of my life,* 104.

7. Gold and Fizdale, 151.

8. *The Morning Post*, London, June 6, 1879.

9. Gold and Fizdale, 126.

Camille Claudel

1. Brigitte Fabre-Pellerin, *Le jour et la nuit de Camille Claudel* (Paris: Lachenal & Ritter, 1988), 58, author's trans.

2. Ibid., 68.

3. Ibid., 51.

4. Reine-Marie de Paris, *The Life of Camille Claudel* (Henry Holt and Company: New York, 1984), 218. Reprinted with permission of the publisher.

5. Odile Ayral-Clause, *Camille Claudel* (New York: Harry N. Abrams, Inc., 2002), 60. Reprinted with permission of the author.

6. *La Presse,* Paris, March 10, 1905.

7. Ayral-Clause, 136.

8. Fabre-Pellerin, 238–239, author's trans.

9. Ibid., 240.

Maria Sklodowska / Marie Curie

1. Susan Quinn, *Marie Curie* (New York: Simon & Schuster, 1995; copyright © 1995 by Susan Quinn), 115. Reprinted with the permission of Simon & Schuster, Inc.

2. Ibid., 156.

3. Eve Curie, *Madame Curie* (Paris: Gallimard, 1938), 298–299, author's trans.

4. Quinn, 127.

5. Ibid., 194.

6. Ibid., 279–280.

7. Ibid., 246.

8. Ibid., 328.

9. Ibid., 285.

Sidonie-Gabrielle Colette

1. Madeleine Lazard, *Colette* (Paris: Gallimard, 2008), 71, author's trans.

2. Colette, *Claudine en ménage*, author's trans.

3. Colette, *Chéri,* author's trans.

Gabrielle "Coco" Chanel

1. Valerie Steele, *Paris Fashion* (New York: Oxford University Press, 1988), 227. By permission of Oxford University Press, Inc.

Simone de Beauvoir

1. From "The Talk of the Town," *The New Yorker*, Vol. XXIII, #1, February 22, 1947, 19–20.

2. Jacques Deguy and Sylvie Le Bon de Beauvoir, *Simone de Beauvoir: écrire la liberté* (Paris: Découvertes Gallimard Litératures), 27, author's trans.

3. Toril Moi, *Simone de Beauvoir* (Paris: Diderot Editeur, 1995), 100, author's trans.

4. Simone de Beauvoir, *La Force des Choses* (Paris: Gallimard, 1963), 211, author's trans.

5. Alice Jardine, February 20, 2009, at the Harvard Humanities Conference for the Simone de Beauvoir centennial.